Sex Positions For Couples

Improve Your Sex Life in Your Relationship or Marriage with Kama Sutra for Beginners Complete with Illustrations and a New Position to Try Everyday

Jenny Love

© **Copyright 2021 by Jenny Love - All rights reserved.**

This document is geared towards providing exact and reliable information in regard to the topic and issue covered.

- From a Declaration of Principles which was accepted and approved equally by a Committee of the American Bar Association and a Committee of Publishers and Associations.

In no way is it legal to reproduce, duplicate, or transmit any part of this document in either electronic means or in printed format. All rights reserved.

The information provided herein is stated to be truthful and consistent, in that any liability, in terms of inattention or otherwise, by any usage or abuse of any policies, processes, or directions contained within is the solitary and utter responsibility of the recipient reader. Under no circumstances will any legal responsibility or blame be held against the publisher for any reparation, damages, or monetary loss due to the information herein, either directly or indirectly.

Respective authors own all copyrights not held by the publisher.

The information herein is offered for informational purposes solely and is universal as so. The presentation of the information is without contract or any type of guarantee assurance.

The trademarks that are used are without any consent, and the publication of the trademark is without permission or backing by the trademark owner. All trademarks and brands within this book are for clarifying purposes only and are owned by the owners themselves, not affiliated with this document.

Table of Contents

Introduction 1

Intimacy, Seduction, and Communication 5

Pre-Sex 13

Easy Sex Positions 21

Intermediate Sex Position 31

Advanced Positions 35

Sex Positions for Pregnant Women 43

Oral Sex for Woman 55

Oral Sex Tips to Drive Her Crazy 61

Oral Sex Tips to Drive Him Crazy 69

Achieving Orgasm 77

Men's Orgasm 85

Women's Orgasm 89

Tips and Tricks (How to last Longer) 95

How Can Sex Toys Improve Your Sex Life? 101

How to Boost Your Sexual Performance 107

Advanced Tips 113

Being Sexual Without Doing It 119

Sexual Energy 127

Tell Your Partner Your Fantasies 133

Your Path to Passion 137

Improve Sexual Libido Adding Hypnosis Session 143
Conclusion...151

Introduction

There are different sex positions for couples that are difficult, and you might not want to try them without someone who has a lot of experience, but if you really want to try these sex positions, then here are some for you to try out if your partner is willing to.

Practicing different sex positions allows couples to have more intimate lovemaking and brings them to orgasm. Many couples have difficulty when having sex because they are not holding each other in many of the sex positions.

Having a pleasurable sex life is essential to anyone, and if you are a couple who lacks in that matter, then it is very important that you have your own sex position for the couple because it doesn't only help your partner, but it also increases your self-pleasure as well.

There are some positions where the moans and groans are heard outside the room because the couple is also experiencing the best head and body contact, which also allows the partner to have better pleasure in a sexual manner and it helps the partner achieve the best orgasms.

Many people are thinking about which positions are good for first-time sex. There are also sex positions for couples who enjoy kissing each other passionately. For those who have no idea about some of the basic sex positions for couples to try out, then you should make sure that you start by learning the basics before you start to try out such sex positions as intercourse.

Your sex life is very important to you; making your sexual life a lot of fun is the best way to start every day, and here are some recommendations for you to try out next.

There are different positions that you can try out with your partner while having sex. One thing that you will notice is that some couples have to worry about their health since they do not know how to have sex properly since they have no idea on the best sex positions for couples at all.

Some benefits of having a good sex life include that it also helps you to relieve stress, it can also help you to improve the performance of your body and it also improves your immune system as well. While having sex with your partner, you should make sure that you have a good understanding of how it is done properly.

In addition, these sex positions for couples are very beneficial to your body because if you are doing the missionary sex position with your partner then it will allow you to get the deepest penetration possible.

In order to make sure that the penetration is deep and pleasurable, you and your partner should try out the position, right angle variation. By doing this you will also be able to enjoy your partner from the back as well as from the front.

It will make you feel very comfortable, and it will also allow you to feel very happy and relieved from the fact that you are able to have the best sex life possible with your partner. It will help you to improve your sexual positions, your love life, and your relationship as well. As the name suggests you need to have sex to reproduce the offspring and for your partner to give you the best pleasure as well as the best orgasms possible.

Making the body more flexible is a good thing to do for sure. Some couples do not know how they can loosen their hips because they do not pay attention to their own body in this regard.
For couples, this is good since it allows them to improve their love life and make sure that they have a pleasurable sex life.

Intimacy, Seduction, and Communication

While we have briefly touched on communication, we are going to look at it much more closely. The level of communication you hold with your partner, friends, and family members is critical in having a healthy outcome. Knowing how to communicate and express yourself is crucial in avoiding toxic relationships.

You will also gain valuable information on how to choose a partner that is going to be good for you. Finding the right person can be difficult. This is especially true when you start to think about the volume of people that are on this planet. You don't need to be intimidated; instead, you need to be educated on what it takes to find the person that is good for you. Likewise, to find the person that you are good for.

Most people understand that for a relationship to be successful you need to be able to communicate with one another. There will never be a perfect relationship; they all go through rough periods. Communication can make these rough patches much easier to deal with. With solid communication skills, you will be able to build a long-lasting, healthy relationship instead of one that tears you both apart.

So, what exactly is communication? Communication is the sharing of information from one component to another. It is what allows us to tell our partner what we are feeling, what we want, and what we need. It is helpful in making sure both parties' needs are met and that there is a true connection within the relationship.

When you are in a relationship, you need to be able to talk to each other about everything. Sure, sometimes it is uncomfortable, but you must remember that people do not mind readers so, you must tell your partner what is going on. The truth can be hard to hear sometimes; however, healthy relationships are built on these sometimes-difficult truths.

You must also remember that misunderstandings happen. To avoid misunderstandings, you need to think before you speak so that you are communicating clearly. Misunderstandings in communication can lead to a person's feeling of being hurt. It could also cause anger or resentment. Obviously, these are all feelings that we want to avoid. This is especially true when dealing with a partner whom you truly love.

Obviously, if you are in a relationship, there are two sides that need to be addressed. The two of you may communicate in very different ways. This can be troublesome all in itself; however, spending the time to understand your partner and how they communicate can make it much simpler. The communication tactics that you use in every relationship in your life could be wildly different. You need to practice talking to the people that you love and allow them to talk to you.

When you are working on communication, you want to remember to state things clearly. It can be hard to understand what people are trying to say. It can be advantageous to write your thoughts and feelings down prior to trying to talk about them. This can give you a clear path toward whatever it is that you are trying to express, and it can help promote understanding from the other person.

In today's world; life can be very busy. Between text messages, emails, children, friends, and family, finding the time to devote to talking with your partner can be difficult. However, it is extremely important to remember to set time aside that is devoted to communication. Remove the distractions and focus on the person you are talking to. This means you should shut off the TV, set the cell phones aside, and make sure you are in a space that is free from interruptions.

Effective communication will consist of telling your partner how what is happening around is affecting you. It should be full of "I" statements so that they can understand your wants, needs, and feelings. You must also remember to take accountability for your feelings. At the same time, no one can tell you how you feel, you do need to understand that sometimes our own heads get in the way of what is truly going on. So, knowing how your surrounding affects your emotions can help lead to better communication.

You should also remember that there is a time and a place for everything. You don't want to call your partner out in a public situation just because you are feeling some type of way. If you do, understand that it can lead to resentment and other ill-feelings toward you from your partner.

Listening is another huge piece of effective communication. You must always remember it is not only about you but also about your partner. Setting your thoughts and feelings to the side and being open to what your partner has to say is critical in great communication skills. This can be one of the harder pieces to learn. You expect that they are going to hear from you, so, in turn, you need to work on actually hearing what it is that they have to say.

Communication is not only about the negative things that are going on in your life or your relationship. Excellent communication will include conversations about good things. Making sure they understand why you appreciate them and how important they are in your life is just as important as letting them know what it is that is bugging you.

You need to keep in mind that when we talk there is more than the simple words we are saying. The tone of your voice will play a major role in how you are expressing yourself. If your words are sharp and loud, your partner is going to think you are angry with them when really you may just be excited. Taking note of your tone can help keep arguments at bay and ensure that the communication continues to flow.

The tone is not the only thing to keep in mind. People communicate verbally, sure, but did you know that we also communicate in a non-verbal fashion? What our bodies are saying is equally as important as what our mouths are saying. This encompasses your posture, inflection, tone, facial expressions, and more.

For example, if you are entering into a conversation with your arms crossed in front of your chest, you are going to be appeared to be closed off to what your partner has to say. This can be intimidating and make it impossible for your partner to express themselves. Instead, put your arms to your sides and relax. This will show them that you are open to communication and will actively listen to what they have to say.

It's funny; more often than not, it is the non-verbal clues that actually show us what people are thinking and feeling. Our body language should reflect the things we are saying. If it does not, your partner is sure to pick up on it. So, it is important that you mean the things that you say and that you pay attention to what your body language is pushing forth.

People have a really hard time remembering that everyone is wrong on occasion. It is completely acceptable to not be right all the time. Having the ability to let things go when they aren't major problems is important. Additionally, understanding that sometimes we must agree to disagree is imperative. We will not always see things eye to eye, and that is totally ok.

Active listening is another huge component of communication. When you an active listener, your partner will be more likely to actually engage with you. Here are some things to show, then you are present and listening:

- Maintain eye contact
- Lean in toward the speaker
- Don't get defensive
- Keep a relaxed posture
- Face the person you are speaking with
- Stay on the same level as they are; if they are sitting, you should be too if they are standing, the same applies
- Try not to fidget; it can be very distracting
- Do not interrupt
- Genuinely pay attention
- Maintain awareness of your tone
- Don't be afraid to step away and come back to a difficult situation/conversation; heightened emotions can break communication down quickly

Maintaining good communication in a relationship will take work. It does not come naturally or easily for many people. Be patient with yourself and the ones that you love. Their feelings matter, as do yours.

If you are someone that struggles with communication or you are in a relationship with someone who does, there are many things that you can do to work on it. Learning better communication skills is always worth the time and will have a positive impact on all of the relationships you are involved in whether they are romantic or not.

Be aware that while some people are great at listening, it does not mean they are great at talking. It can be very hard for some people to find the right words to express themselves effectively. Some people can only express themselves with their actions until they start to focus on learning communication techniques.

If you are trying to help your partner communicate more effectively there are absolutely some things you can do to help them along the way. Some things you can do to help your partner communicate are:

- Be open and honest with them. Share your thoughts, experiences, concerns, and ideas. This should be done with an appreciation of them listening.
- Show them affection and praise them when they discuss things with you openly.
- Help them look at the important issues you are both facing. This includes things like goals, parenting styles, and finances.
- Comfort your partner when they are feeling down or if you see they need it. This type of intimate attention can make communication seem easier.

- Encourage them to talk about what they are feeling on a daily basis. Sometimes the simple feelings are the best place to start.

These are only a few of the many ways you can encourage communication. Know that it is a two-way street so, you will also need to work on your communication skills. When you are committed to someone and want to sustain a healthy relationship, it really all comes down to communication.

Communication can be easier with some people than with others. Part of good communication is choosing the right partner. Some find that they don't really have a choice in who they fall in love with; however, you can take steps to ensure you are choosing a mate that is healthy for you.

When you are choosing a partner, you should find someone who tells you exactly who they are as a person. Most relationships go through a honeymoon period where we try to show our best selves. This can actually be detrimental due to the fact it is an unrealistic representation of who the person really is. When you meet someone that lays it all out in the beginning, it makes it simpler to know exactly what you are getting into.

When you do find the person who will tell you exactly who they are, you need to listen. Never move forward with the belief you can change someone. People can only change themselves. If you have this mind frame, you are setting yourself and your relationship up for failure.

Pre-Sex

How to Prepare for Great Sex

Basically, if you want to make sure that the sexual experience of your partner with you is just as pleasant as your sexual personality, then there are additional things you need to know to make the encounter a pleasurable and appealing one.

- **Shower Yourself Properly**

It is always best to wash properly, and pay close attention to your arms, the pubic region, and between your thighs. Take a moment to wash your entire body properly with plain water first when showering, and do not use soap or shower gels during this initial process. After you have a feeling that your face, vagina, and anus have been rubbed off with a lot of sweat, sticky stuff, and slimy things, you may then continue to use soap on your body.

Women should wash their outer genital areas and anus properly during the shower. This will undoubtedly help avoid yeast infections and remove bad odor. Nonetheless, women shouldn't aggressively wash their pussy or lace it with any scented liquids as this can affect the vagina's pH balance and make it vulnerable to vaginal infections. This would also contribute to the same stinky smell you're trying to get rid of your pussy first, and probably pass the infection to the cock of your friend. You should also make sure you dry your pussy gently and don't attempt to rub it harshly with a towel.

On the other hand, and, by beginning at the head of the penis, men must properly clean their cock, because (in mostly circumcised men) the head of the cock will come into direct contact with sweat, and bacteria. This can quickly find its way into a woman's vagina during puberty and later cause a foul-smelling infection with yeast. Uncircumcised men will retreat as far back as possible without causing any pain. This will show both penis glans with some lukewarm water that needs to be gently washed. Hence, men should properly wash their cock to make sure it stays clean, both before and after the sexual act, to prevent infections on themselves or their partner.

- **Switch from Sweaty Underwear, and Clothing**

Getting home from work, shopping, or shopping, and then choosing to stay in your sweaty underwear and clothing are unhealthy. Even if your sweat-drenched underwear or clothing has dried, it can still cause a foul odor to emanate from your pores and also from your vagina or pubic region, which during intercourse can become uncomfortably amplified in its smell.

In fact, sweaty underwear also poses a high risk as bacteria and yeast grow wondrously in sweat, which can then lead to infection of the urinary tract or yeast.

Sweat and flowing dirt may also block the skin pores around the pubic area and cause folliculitis, which is an inflammation, and hair follicle infection around the pussy, and eventual outer vagina infection once the sweat streams to your panty liner or underwear.

Simply put, therefore, if you expect sex immediately after boring housework, an err, and, or a sweaty journey, —you should try to make sure your clothes are loosened as quickly as possible afterward, and if necessary, remove your underwear for a while or change it altogether.

Another choice is to quickly rush into the bathroom and give your pussy a good wash in preparation for waiting home for your man. I would warn you, though, to be vigilant about doing this as soon as you get home, or even a little while later. Because your man may think the pussy went cheating, and you just choose to freshen it up from that. Ha! Yea! Ha! Yea!

- **Armpit, and Pubic hair cleanliness**

The sweat glands under your axis offer a fouler smell than any other part of your body. It would, therefore, get quickly inundated with an unpleasant odor before and during sex. As such, you can make sure before sex, it is fully shaved and deodorized. Likewise, for a few good reasons, you can ensure your pussy (or pubic area) is well shaved. A rasped pubic region gives a nice hygienic look to your pussy, also eliminates scratching and bad odor. After all, it's not only humiliating to have your vagina blocked out by a forest that surrounds your butt, but it's disgraceful to have a pubic farm that develops parasites while producing a foul smelly waterfall.

Essentially, the pubic region is not properly exposed to fresh air. As such, it becomes practically a boiling pot for pathogens as heat and sweat make bacteria perfect breeding ingredients. Always ensure that you take some time off to keep your armpit, male pubic, and the pussy section rasped and washed.

- **Deal with the Washroom Early**

It can really be a turn-off if you unexpectedly must shove your guy off you or jump off his cock so that you can quickly get to the washroom to urinate or defecate to prevent vomiting on yourself. So, girls, if you feel like urinating before the action or even during the foreplay, please ask for an excuse, and make sure your bladder is drained or defecated, then clean and wash your anus properly. Never stick to the urge to go urinating in the washroom, particularly before sex.

Urinating will allow your bladder to rid your urinary tract of the bacteria and contaminants that grow. Delaying urination can speed up the breeding of bacteria that leads to urethra (and vagina) infections of a woman or the cock of your partner. So again, remembering the washroom before they get into practice is perfect for males and females alike. The washroom can also make the woman's needs likely to give a quick rinse to her sweaty cunt, and the man's cock a refreshed clean for the next dose of oral sex.

- **Clean your Mouth**

Usually, the mouth is the first fluid-flowing contact organ for two people about to engage in sexual intercourse. A mouth that tastes like overnight piss, or a slimy mouth, and packed with stuck food, will be a turn off to be accepted. Until going on a sex escapade, it is always best to brush your teeth again or use mouthwash until interfacing with your friend.

A nice breath and clean mouth would cause some cool and sexy kisses that would, in effect, heat the moment in preparation for good sex.

- **Clean your Insertion toys, and Finger**

Fingering a woman before sex is one of the most thrilling and sexually charged things that a man can do if he does it correctly, but if you're going to use sex toys, fondle yourself or let your man caress the cunt, please make sure the toys are washed and cleaned, and the fingers (and fingernails) of your man are clean.

While women take their time off to get a daily manicure, care for their nails, and to keep it clean, men don't put that much effort into it, even though their nails would have become unclean and clogged with hard-working infectious dirt, etc.

Many people have a history of not paying much attention to their bodies and would often leave their hygienic needs in a state of neglect. As such, a single man's fingernail will contain more bacteria and germs than the rest of his whole body and your body put together.

And if you allow him to insert a disgusting, bacteria-infested fingernail into your cunt, he could insert a good one of those bad species that can give you a good dose of yeast infection and a robust and foul-smelling vagina afterward. Then, you can make sure his fingers are dry, or remind him to wash his h, and properly, and under his nails, because you won't want to regret the fun a week or so later.

Pre-sex Safety Measures

While you can do your best to ensure that the hygienic standards are in place for good sex, there are some other items you need to remember secretly until you get into action. Such issues can have long-term effects on your health, your protection, and overall well-being, being, specifically, if you engage with multiple sex partners or work outside a committed relationship (or marriage).

1. Do not carelessly consent to have sex (including oral) without a condom unless the person with whom you have sex is your husband/wife or partner in a long-term, committed relationship because people aren't as often as innocent as they might seem. Typically, asking a partner to consent to a joint HIV and other STD tests is hard, if not nearly

impossible. Usually, they will accuse you of not trusting them, or in fact, even you might fear a check. But I do not see why a fair man or woman should disagree with a check for HIV. That aside, some people build trust in the other person subconsciously, after having sexual intercourse two or three times, or after being convinced otherwise., but as the saying goes, -It is up to you to decide if you want to spend a moment of fun for a horror lifetime. In other cases, before the sexual activity, and HIV and/or STD test would not have been practically possible. Condoms can also prevent unwanted abortions and a long list of other illnesses that are sexually transmitted.

However, do not conduct oral sex if either partner has sores inside the mouth or around the genitals as this may lead to infections or maybe a symptom of an existing infection.

2. Do not consent to premature sexual intercourse, oral sex, and anal sex unless you are comfortable. Still, if you are against this in a long-term relationship or marriage that can be troublesome. You'd have to figure out that with your partner in some way.

In other cases, most people wouldn't feel physically fulfilled even at one-night stands when oral sex is offered or provided.

3. Be careful with the food or the drink you are given; one of the risks involved in looking for sex outside of a committed relationship may be that you are secretly given inducement drugs in your drink, and food, etc. To do things you wouldn't usually have wanted to do during intercourse. Therefore, avoiding alcoholic beverages or other consumption deals may be a good idea if you're about to have sex with an abusive spouse or someone you're involved in a premature relationship, including first-time timers.

4. Make sure your partner understands your sexual needs and preferences before you agree to romp in bed with him or her. After all, if an animalistic man felt you were too uptight, you wouldn't want your

interaction to turn into a date rape of your anus, etc. So, make your sexual preference very clear, particularly in first-time encounters, before you indulge.

5. Do not allow your partner to photograph or record under any circumstances, in the nude or any sexual position, particularly in premature relations. This may take less than five minutes for someone to post a nude photo of you on the internet or share it with others, who may bring you a lifetime of humiliation if the picture is manipulated or shared without your permission. You should also be mindful of the pressure your partner puts on having sex in one place or condition that may compromise your privacy.

While this measure may well sit with younger partnerships, married couples and those in long-term relationships tend to allow for their private perusal of photography. Please ensure that in such a case, you have 100 percent confidence in your partner even to consider such an idea. After all, while it may now seem like a cool thing, it may turn out later to be a deplorable idea.

Easy Sex Positions

Kneeling

Many couples prefer to have sex on their knees as it is comfortable as well as enthusiastic. In these positions, both the partners lie closer with one or both on the knees, allowing enough room for the other to settle down and enjoy the exposure of the bodily parts. These positions allow both partners to set the pace of sexual intercourse, controlling the deepness of the penetration. If you want real enjoyment with the touch of sensation, you must try these positions with your partners to get out of the box enjoyment and satisfaction from sex. Key conditions for good sex are the ability to get more out of it and try and experimenting with the most daring fantasies to explore and expose the holes of your female partner and satisfy her with your fullness. Being a ruler in sex demands nothing more than just passion and deliverance.

Saint

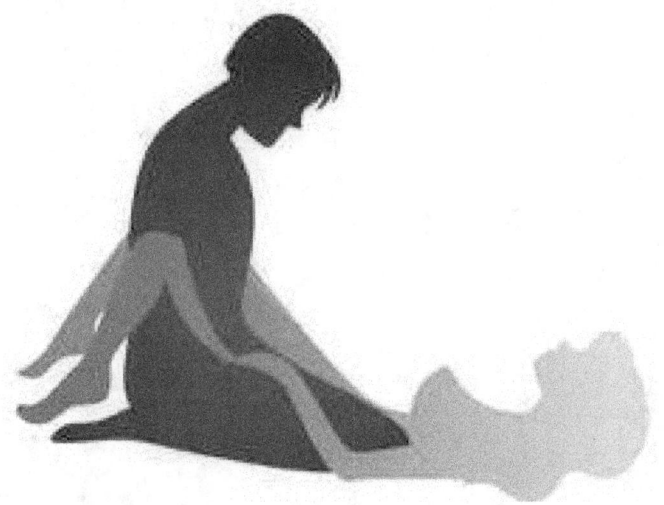

This is one of the favorable positions of the kneeling family as it offers an explorative approach towards the holes together with fishy movements. The standard variation of this family has the man sitting while kneeling backward and the woman lying with her back on the floor and the lower part of her body lying on his lap with knees folded upward. This position allows access to both holes together with the intent of going slower or a bit harsher according to the choice of both partners. Both partners are face-to-face, providing enough opportunity for kissing, licking, or boobs sucking, together with the option of body licking for the woman too. The woman on her knees mat fastens the mobility. Otherwise, speedy penetration isn't guaranteed. But the thing that is ensured is a deeper penetration with strong clitoral stimulation together with intense rubbing when going curvy inside the vaginal or anal hole. Moving on while rotating the hips, also helped by the man with his hands on her hips, could make the sex more enjoyable and enthusiastic. Mildness comes naturally by going harsh.

Kneeling Saint

This is quite an amazing sex position as it offers more divine and enthusiastic sex, giving intense hugging experiences. The woman with folded knees sits on his lap while hugging him deeply and kissing him with her full. On the other hand, the man with folded knees sits on the floor while making room for her on his lap and hugging her intensely, kissing her face and sucking her boobs with his full. This position, with enough kissing and hugging experiences, becomes the favorite and enjoyable for many people who love to indulge deeply in sex. Another fiesta is the position of the vagina that lies right in front of the man's penis, allowing frictionless inclusion with curvy angles. These penetration angles happen with more rubbing, stimulating wild sex and allow to go deep inside the vaginal hole. The anal inclusion isn't guaranteed a bit deep as the anal hole isn't as near as the vaginal hole. But the anal gaping, together with friction to the walls of the anus, might turn both partners into wild beasts by going harsher and slightly slap on her ass.

Pressed Guard

Another folded knees sex position from the family of kneeling sex positions is pressed guard. In this position, the woman presses her knees on the man's chest and allows him frictionless access to her holes by putting both the holes right in front of the man's penis. The woman lies on the floor with her back while the man sits on his knees and lifts her ass by putting his hands beneath her ass. This lets him go deep and straight into her vaginal and anal hole as both the holes allow their access. Normally, this position involves deeper penetration with a harsher approach, but the woman can control the inclusion by pressing on her chest if she feels pain due to the harsh approach. This position also possesses a drawback that if the woman loses her control due to mildness and wild attitude, it could kick off on his face or might push him backward. The better options could be to explore the holes and enjoy the feelings by tilting, changing angles, and letting the partner take over.

Bent Guard

It involves the woman lying on the floor with her back and ass up in her partner's lap and feet on his chest by bending the knees, allowing him to stay in control and have fun with her holes. On the other hand, the man is sitting on his knees while leaning a bit forward and allowing her eye contact. This position involves better angles and better sex with easy penis inclusion into the vagina and anal hole. Man can go deep with harsh intent and use force to tighten her legs and feel the heat of the moment. He can also raise the sensation and joys by slapping her a bit on her ass, with her accordance. The woman could feel every inch of his penis when included in the anal hole with the use of force and rubbing her gaping. More friction involves when the penis goes into the vagina, resulting in a strong stimulation and greater orgasms for her. The experience of sex would be quite sensational and fantastic with higher satisfaction up to offloading for both partners.

Folded Guard

Another interesting position in the family of kneeling sex positions. It allows the woman to lie on the floor with her shoulders and her pelvis lifted by the man with his hands beneath her buttocks and her legs up in the air, hanging on his shoulders. This position offers greater mobility with a large area of skin touching each other and making physical contact sensational by praising the partner. The woman being lifted off the ground and her holes right in front of his penis invite his penis to go deep and mobilize her body by doing fast in and out from the vagina or anal hole. Anal sex could be a lot sensational and enthusiastic as the anal hole allows straight inclusion and turns the sex into a mild experience. While going into the vagina could be a curvy inclusion as pussy lies a bit higher than the penis, guaranteeing more rubbing and more gentle experience by using slight force, pushing her forward by the man. This position could be tried with some tilt and angles to get the most out of it.

Bent Candle

The bent candle is another sex position in the family of kneeling sex positions. This position is known all over the world and very appreciated by couples. In this position, the woman lies on the ground with her back touching the ground and her legs up in the air, hanging straight up with the body of her partner. On the other hand, the man is standing on her knees with his legs folded and hands on the knees of his female partner, holding her tightly to support her legs and making room for his penis in her pelvis. The woman is lying straight on the ground with face and boobs up, enthusiasting him to kiss and fuck thoroughly. The sex would be quite reluctant and sensational as it offers deep penetration with straight and curvy inclusion inside the vaginal and anal hole, allowing both partners to move fast or slow according to their choice. The man could go gently and slower, if he wants, to feel the sensations and satisfy his partner by offloading her from cum, whereas, he may go hard to feel the heat of the moment.

Folded Candle

The folded candle is much similar to the bent candle. It also offers the woman lying with a straight back on the ground and her legs straighten up in the air, touching the body of the man and giving him enormous exposure of her holes together with the option of choosing any of the holes to go deep. Her legs are slightly folded and leaned forward towards her abdomen. While the man is behind her pelvis, standing on kneeling knees and holding her buttocks and thighs with his hands to pull her towards himself to guarantee deep penetration. This position allows him to expose both of the holes and go deep into the vaginal hole as the vagina is pretty much right in front of his penis and waiting for the shattering of a cock. The anal hole is a bit beneath the penis as her pelvis is lifted by the man above the ground. Therefore, it favors the anal gaping and makes it sensational, together with strong clitoral stimulation by rubbing the penis with the inner lips of the vagina.

Tilted Candle

Another enthusiastic position in the family of kneeling sex positions is the tilted candle. In this position, the woman lies on the ground with her shoulders and head rested on the ground. While his lower part is lifted above the ground by the man with his hands beneath her buttocks. The woman places both of her legs on the same side of the man, leaving her a bit imbalanced. This position offers the man a lot more creativity to fasten his strokes as he has more room for his penis to strike hard to reach the depths of the vagina. In this way, he can make sex really hard for the woman and make him immediately offloading with cum and satisfying her completely. The best approach to enjoy this position is to raise her pelvis up and tilt her lower body to make room for the penis and exposure. Trying all angles of this position can offer to explore the beauties of sex, either going gentle or harsh, relying on mutual understanding.

Split Kneeling

The position is quite similar for both partners. The woman is standing on a knee, touching the ground while another crossing with the knee of the man. The male partner is also standing in an identical situation. This position offers both partners the sensations of the sex on their knees while holding each other tightly. The man holds her buttocks to push her forward and hug her tightly to ingest her boobs in his chest and feel the heat of the moment. The female partner hugs him tightly with her hands around his neck and rests her head on his shoulder. The man can go forward with powerful strikes to hit deep inside her vaginal hole and to ensure strong clitoral stimulation. Whereas, to go deep inside the anal hole, he must lift her a bit to make penis inclusion possible. Going inside the anal hole could be a lot difficult but quite amazing and sensational due to its enjoyment factor.

Intermediate Sex Position

The Lotus Position

This is a position that requires patience and practice; however, it is rewarding once you get used to it. The lotus involves one partner (usually male) seated on a firm but soft surface, such as a bed or soft rug, with his legs folded (or cross-legged). As he becomes erect, his partner (usually female) will slowly descend onto him, with both feet placed firmly next to him so she can softly land onto him as he slips inside. Once both are fully settled into this position, the woman's arms and legs are wrapped around the man, and he reciprocates with a similar embrace. This is a deeply intimate pose. The couple can look into each other's eyes at close proximity and embrace during the full experience of lovemaking. The woman can slightly lift and adjust within the position to gain a slightly different angle, which can allow her to experience more pleasure and possibly orgasm. To make this a successful pose, use a lot of lubrication and take it slow. This is not a position that accommodates a quick motion or thrust but rather a slower, more tantric pace.

The Butterfly

  This position is a fun and ambitious pose that requires a bit of flexibility. In this pose, the man is standing, while the woman is lying on her back with her legs held in the air, though not too far apart, so as to be able to place each one on her partner's shoulders. In doing this, the man can easily penetrate and gently push against his partner's legs as he enters deeper.

This position gives the man a full view of the woman as he penetrates her; he can be standing at the edge of the bed during this process or with legs bent on the bed in the same fashion. For some women, keeping their legs slightly bent makes the transition into this position easier until they become more comfortable.

Three-Legged Dog

This position is done standing up, usually with one partner against a wall for added support and one leg raised so that the partner can easily enter and penetrate. It is not the easiest feat to pull off, though it is fun despite the challenge and can be done in a variety of places. For the woman, having her back against the wall is a good support during this pose. Moreover, lifting one leg can be done with some support; the man holds and positions the lifted leg slightly higher or to the side so that he can enter easily. There is a bit of fine-tuning that involves figuring out at which angle is best to enter. Another variable to consider is the height of both individuals. If one person is taller (the male), it may be easier to enter when the woman is standing on a support or at a higher level. Alternatively, the male can bend or maneuver his position to lower his stance and accommodate a different height. This three-legged dog works easiest for people who are similar in height, though it can be achievable for anyone if you are willing to get creative and flexible (Emery, 2018).

The Hot Seat

This position involves the man sitting in a kneeling position with his upper body leaning back, allowing for his partner, facing in the same direction and knelt in the same fashion, and slipping her legs in between his, which are apart enough to enter inside from behind. As she leans back, they become closer, with his arms wrapping around her torso as she reaches for his waist from behind. This position works well in a slow, steady motion.

Advanced Positions

The Head Rush

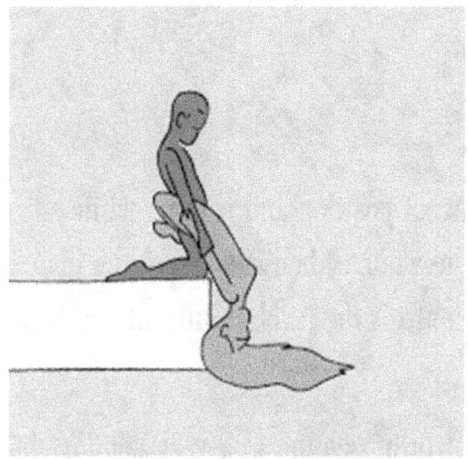

This position requires the man to move to the edge of the bed with his upper body off of the bed and preferably resting on the floor. The woman then takes her position on top. This position is called the Head Rush because the extended length of time in this position will literally make the man's blood rush to his head, effecting a head rush. This could also refer to the case of blood rushing to both his "heads."

Face Off

This is a very erotic sexual position and is done while sitting on a chair or on the edge of the bed. The woman then sits facing the man and wraps her arms around his back, and controls the level of intensity of thrusts by riding up and down the male shaft.

This allows for a lot of intimacy and is a very comfortable position that will allow long, drawn-out sex sessions.

This is also called the Lap Dance.

The Pole Position

This is a slight variation of the reverse cowgirl but will require a little bit more effort from the man as he has to keep one leg outstretched in the air. The woman then assumes the position and grabs hold of the outstretched thigh as a means of dual support.

This is also known as the Thighmaster.

The One Up

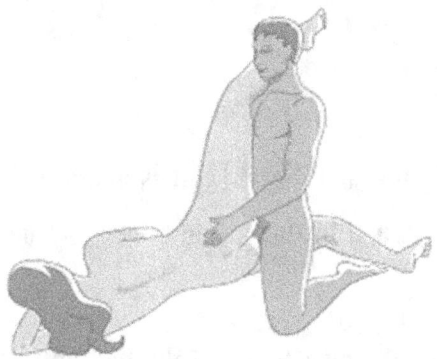

Every woman's vagina and clitoris are unique. This, therefore, means that there are varying levels of sensitivity for women. This sexual position is targeted towards women who have a particular sensitivity to one side of their clitoris.

This requires having the woman lie on the edge of the bed with one leg raised, supported by wrapping her hands around her hamstring just below the knee. This will allow her to have more control of her hip movements and it can assist you in locating the perfect spot to achieve maximum stimulation.

The Spider

This may sound a little bit complicated but is actually very easy to perform. What this will require is a little bit of choreography between you and your partner.

What this requires is for the man to sit on the bed with the woman seated on his lap. The partners face each other with arms back for support. Now here's the complicated part: you will have to move in time with each other thrusting forward, or you can rock back and forth in unison. This position allows for a very erotic view as the woman has her hips between the man's spread legs with her knees bent and feet outside of his hips. Both partners can maintain eye contact while they are performing this sexual act.

This act is also called the Crab Walk.

Getting a Leg Up

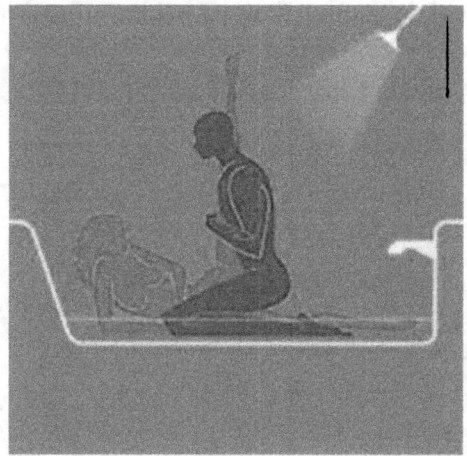

This is a slight modification of the Crab Walk. Instead of the woman's legs spread out on the bed, she lifts these up onto the man's shoulders.

This can lead to very quick orgasms as the woman is able to control her pelvic movements easily.

Bottom's Up

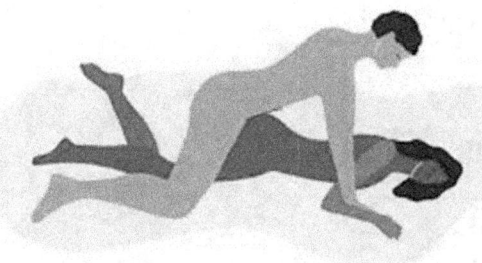

Are you up for a bit of a challenge? Well, here's one! The Bottom's up is a little bit difficult to perform as it requires a little bit of contortionism and athleticism. First, the woman lies on her back, and the man straddles her as she is facing away. Next, she lifts her legs to wrap them around his back and, at the same time, to elevate her pelvic region for easy entry. Last, she then grabs on to the man's buttocks and, with a concerted effort, slides up and back.

You'll have to try it to find out just how pleasurable it is!

Sidewinder

The man and the woman lie on their sides, facing each other. Spreading her legs, the woman allows the man to enter her. In this position, the couple can see each other, and this encourages a lot of physical contact like hugging and kissing.

This is also called the facing spoon.

The Horny Mantis

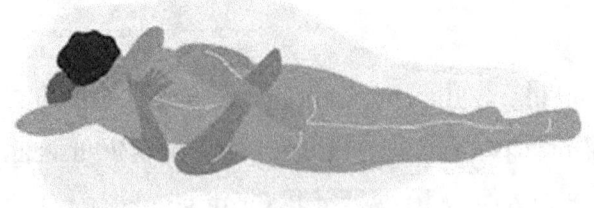

This is a variation of the sidewinder. While in the sidewinder position, the female lifts her leg up and over her partner's body and locks him in place by securing her leg on the man's back. This position allows for deeper penetrations.

The Standing Dragon

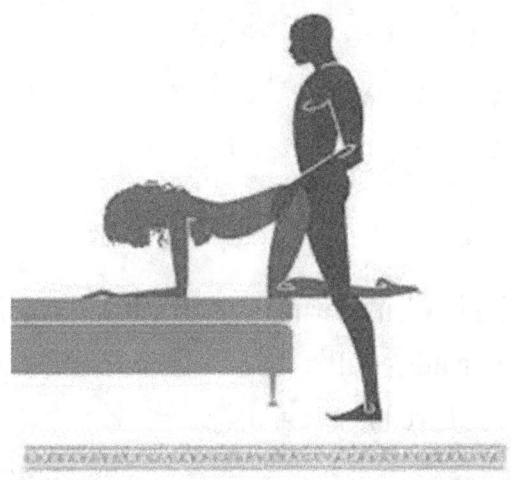

This move is a modified doggy style where the man has to stand while the woman gets on all fours at the edge of the bed. She will have to spread out a little bit more than usual and arch her buttocks more for this position.

Entering from behind, the man gets a very erotic view of her buttocks as he pounds into the woman. Thrusting in this position can be done lightly or as aggressively as the woman wants.

Another fun name for this is the Crouching Tiger, Hidden Serpent.

The X Position

The X position is basically what its name portrays. It will require you and your partner to lie facing each other with your legs forward and over on top of each other. This forms an X, hence the name.

This position is a bit limiting so thrusting is instead replaced with small gyrations which prolong arousal and lead to great orgasms.

Sex Positions for Pregnant Women

For whatever length of time that it's agreeable, put it all on the line!

If you engage in sexual relations, will your growing baby have the option to listen stealthily by the third trimester?

All things considered, sure. In any case, the good news? All sounds are very much suppressed, and your baby can't comprehend filthy talk in any language.

On the other hand, imagine a scenario in which you don't need anything to do with sex. That is typical. It could be anything from your hormones to becoming acclimated to your new body.

"Regularly, the subsequent trimester is the brilliant spot," says Holly Richmond, a clinical sex specialist and authorized marriage and family advisor. The most exceedingly terrible of morning affliction (if you were honored with any) is finished, and you're simply coming into your bends. In the third trimester, a growing belly can begin making sex progressively clumsy.

However, here's the establishment of all that you'll realize with regards to pregnancy sex: All sex is good sex as long as it's pleasurable and consensual.

During pregnancy, you may feel anything from suggestive to exotic or far expelled from needing to have intercourse. Be that as it may, don't fall into the snare of reasoning, it's unrealistic to be pregnant and sexually dynamic.

Adapt precisely having pregnancy sex, from how it feels to how it really influences the baby.

How safe is pregnancy sex?

Unless your primary care physician or midwife has exacting, specific purposes behind you not engaging in sexual relations, it's completely safe — for you, your partner, and your creating baby. (If your PCP or midwife basically says "sex," don't be hesitant to clarify if they mean entrance just or all sexual incitement.)

At present, it is revealed in the information that pregnancy sex isn't merely safe. It's most likely good for you, as well.

Ladies who have climaxes during pregnancy profit by quieting hormones and expanded cardiovascular bloodstream, and those advantages get went down to baby, notes Aleece Fosnight, a doctor collaborator and sex guide in urology, ladies' well-being, and sexual medication.

Here are some insane hot approaches to do it that are 100 percent pregnant-woman affirmed.

The Reclining Goddess

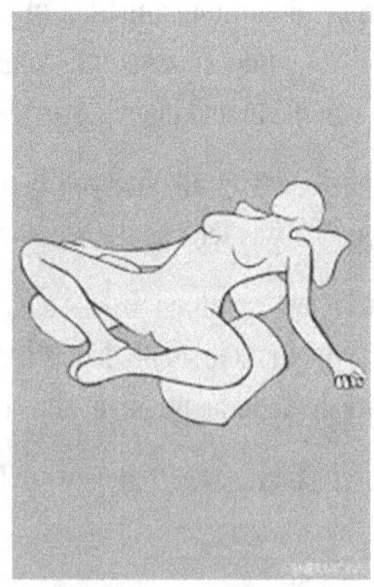

Here's a simple spot to begin. You're going to deliver the supernatural occurrence of life; your partner can welcome the oral sex from this point until your water breaks. Lie on the edge of the bed, have them expect an agreeable position, and find a good pace. Simply ensure they're not blowing air into your vagina.

The Rock Chair Roll

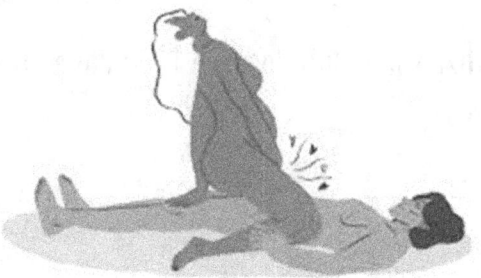

Later on in your pregnancy, you may need to modify lady on-top positions. Have a go at leaning back on your hands to circulate the heaviness of your growing belly and to open up more space for your partner (or you) to invigorate your clit.

Mother Time

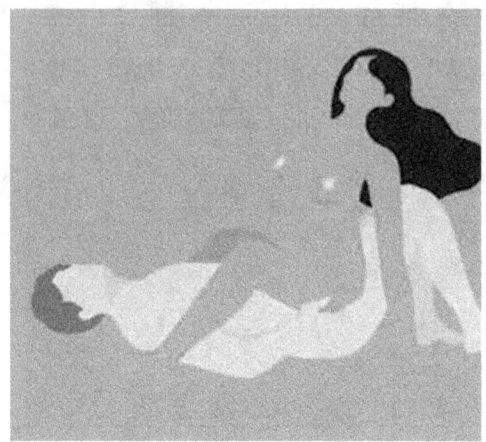

Over the most recent couple of long stretches of pregnancy, you presumably simply need to be spread out the love seat do as well, IT.

Stage 1: Fill your partner's hand with lube and direct it between your legs.

Stage 2: Belatedly realize you didn't do stage 1 ½: Put a towel under your butt for lube drippings.

Bedside Service

Being very comfortable is a top need, so prop yourself up on a huge amount of pads and sit at the edge of the bed, opening your legs wide. Your partner can stop or stand, and alter your pad circumstance for tallness. When you hit an ideal pad position, rub your clit while you both watch their smooth, slow pushes into your stunning, round body. Also, if you can't reach your clit, have them rub it for you.

Three Peas in a Pod

Spooning is a good go-to position during the third trimester on the grounds that your gigantic belly will hinder your love. (This won't be the last time your child does this). To make it stunning: Hold a slug vibrator on your clit by pressing your legs firmly together as your partner rocks into you from behind. No better method to feel both turned on and very much adored than a cuddly spoon fuck.

Bun in the Oven

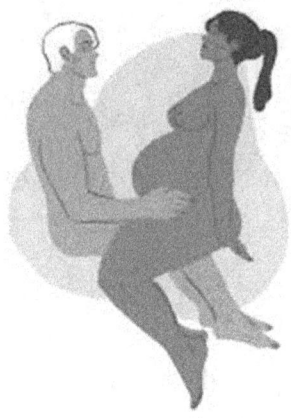

Shouldn't lie on your back a lot during the second and third trimesters, so standard minister is essentially off the table. In any case, if that is your preferred position, turn it on its side by putting a pad under one side of your butt and back. Have him lie confronting you on his side and entwine his legs with yours. If your belly's disrupting the general flow, he can lean his middle away from you and push all the more straight up into you. All the advantages of the husband — that is, you can lie there (during pregnancy this will appear to be tremendously engaging) — without the striking drawback of packing the vena cava, a vein you'll be expected to appropriately Give Life and so forth.

Belly with a View

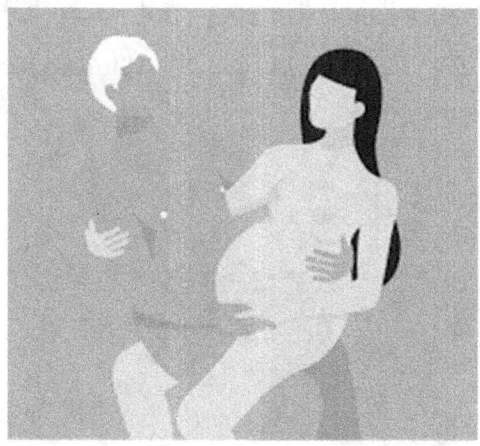

Pregnancy implies heaps of doggy-style sex. Zest-it up by moving to the lounge room and stooping on the love seat, confronting the back. Your partner will likewise be in a fine situation to stretch around and stroke your labia, which—like apparently everything else on your body during these months—is swollen as hellfire. Right now, that is a good thing. Real good. Gracious, you'll see.

Toy Joy

Hard, inner toys like glass and metal can really wound your cervix if pushed in too commandingly, so attempt a clit-centered toy like a Satisfier Pro for delicate suction that feels like oral. Your partner straddles a without hands vibe like Adam and Eve's Ravishing Rabbit Thruster so they can hold your toy set up (you probably won't have the option to reach). You lean back onto a monster heap of cushions and rapture out.

The Boppy Boff

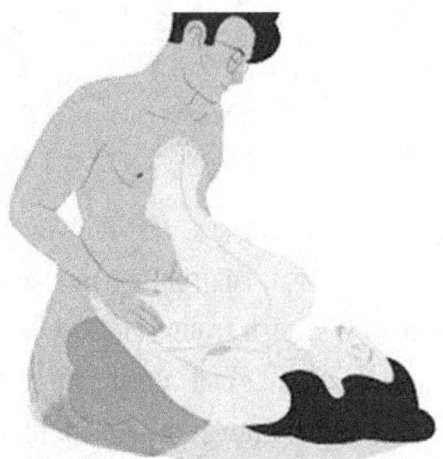

If you are pregnant, somebody will probably gift you a Boppy pad, a C-formed pad that proves to be useful later if you're nursing. Be that as it may, use it off-name now. Lie over it, cautiously accommodating your knock inside the C, so you're not putting your weight on your belly. Your man enters from behind. Never tell your future kid this occurred.

Push It Real Good

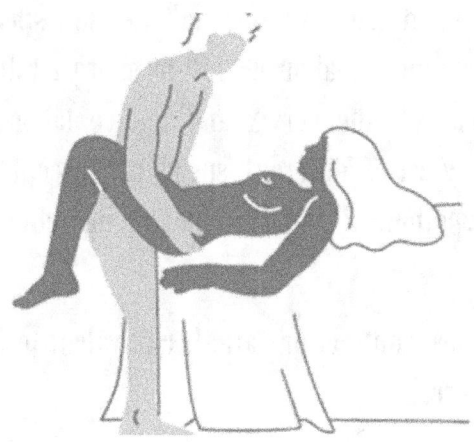

There's a ton about the entire "birthing a youngster" experience that will cause you to feel cruel and undignified (gracious, hold up until you meet the bosom siphon). So grasp your base nature by having his stoop on the bed and sit back on his lap in kind of a bowing converse cowgirl. Groan boisterously and let yourself go wild. Cleansing, and too hot.

Sex After Pregnancy

Pregnant ladies and their accomplices frequently wonder if it's safe to engage in sexual relations during pregnancy.

Is Sex Safe During Pregnancy? (More emphasis)

Infiltration and intercourse's movement won't hurt the infant, who is ensured by your stomach area and the uterus' solid dividers. The amniotic sac's liquid additionally pads your child.

The contractions of climax aren't equivalent to labor contractions. In any case, as a general safety precautionary measure, a few specialists exhort staying away from sex in the last long time of pregnancy, accepting that hormones in semen called prostaglandins can invigorate contractions. One particular case might be for ladies who are late and need to induce labor. A few specialists accept that prostaglandins in semen induce labor in a full-term or past-due pregnancy since the gel used to "mature" the cervix and induce labor likewise contains prostaglandins. In any case, different specialists accept this semen/labor association is just hypothetical and that having intercourse doesn't trigger labor.

Concerning climax, those contractions aren't equivalent to labor contractions. So there's no issue there.

When Not to Have Sex During Pregnancy

Your primary care physician may encourage you not to have intercourse if you have any of the accompanying kinds of high-risk pregnancy:

1. You're at risk for premature delivery or history of past unnatural birth cycles
2. You're at risk for preterm labor (contractions before 37 weeks of pregnancy)
3. You're having a vaginal dying, release, or squeezing without a known reason.
4. Your amniotic sac is releasing liquid or has cracked layers.
5. Your cervix has opened too soon in pregnancy.
6. Your placenta is excessively low in the uterus (placenta previa)
7. You're anticipating twins, triplets, or other "products."

Remember, if your primary care physician says "no sex," that may incorporate whatever includes climax or sexual excitement, not merely intercourse.

Pregnancy Sex

Each lady's encounters during pregnancy are different—including how she feels about sex.

For a few, want blurs during pregnancy. Other ladies feel all the more profoundly associated with their sexuality and progressively excited when they're pregnant.

Is it OK to engage in sexual relations during pregnancy?

Your creating child is secured by the amniotic liquid in your uterus, just as by the solid muscles of the uterus itself. Sexual action won't influence your child, as long as you don't have confusion, for example, preterm labor or placenta issues. In any case, pregnancy can cause changes in your degree of solace and sexual want.

Will Sex During Pregnancy Cause An Unnatural Birth Cycle?
Having intercourse during pregnancy won't incite an unnatural birth cycle. Most unnatural birth cycles happen because the embryo isn't growing typically.

What Are The Best Sexual Positions During Pregnancy?
Oral sex is additionally safe during pregnancy. Let your innovativeness dominate, as long as you remember shared delight and solace.

Are Condoms Essential?
Having a sexually transmitted contamination during pregnancy can cause genuine medical issues for you and your infant. Maintain a strategic distance from all types of sex—vaginal, oral, and butt-centric—if your accomplice has a functioning or, as of late, analyzed sexually transmitted contamination.

Utilize A Condom If
1. You're not in a commonly monogamous relationship. You decide to engage in sexual relations with another accomplice during pregnancy.

2. Are there times when sex ought to be kept away from?
3. Your social insurance supplier may prescribe staying away from sex if:
4. You have unexplained vaginal dying
5. You're releasing amniotic liquid.
6. Your cervix starts to open rashly (cervical inadequacy)
7. You have a past filled with preterm labor or untimely birth.
8. Imagine a scenario where I would prefer not to engage in sexual relations.

That is OK. There's a whole other world to closeness than sex. Offer your needs and worries to your accomplice in an open and cherishing way. If sex is difficult, unappealing, or untouchable, have a go at snuggling, kissing, or back rub.

Oral Sex for Woman

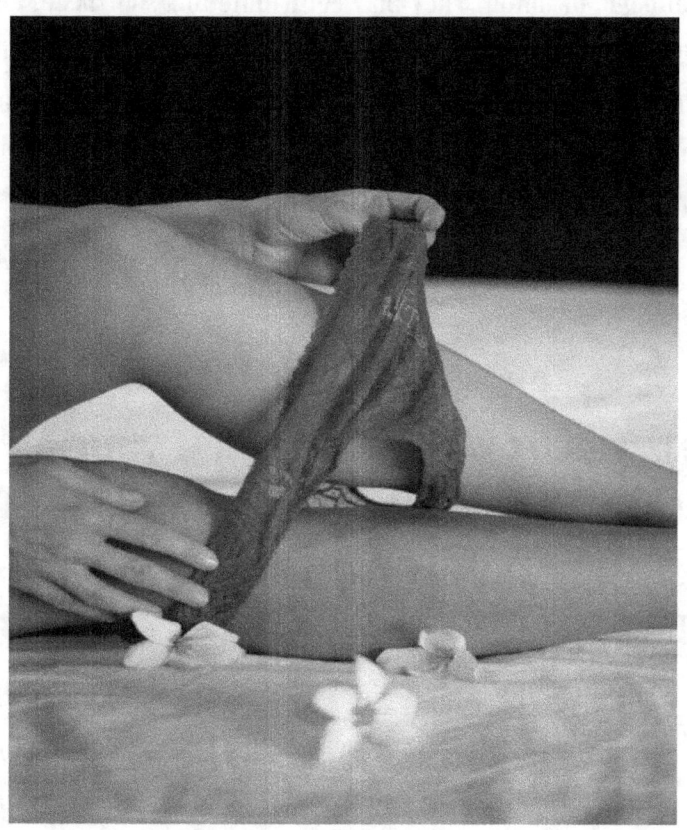

How Would It Taste Like?

Quite frankly, there is no way to generalize the experience of oral sex. Some enjoy it a lot, and others, the other way. It can heighten the excitement in your body during sex. It can also be grouped as strong seduction foreplay that could turn your partner on. All that is apart from its role as a direct substitute to penile-vagina penetration. In case you are still wondering what it tastes likes, it is amazing! Every human has got a personal taste down there, you shouldn't hope to meet a garden rose smell too, but be sure it is amazing.

The joy lies in watching your partner's face flicker with pure sensation as your flip your tongue on their clit or penis. If you are looking forward to oral sex sometimes, you can improve your body's taste by steering clear of foods like asparagus, cabbage, or onion. They may contribute to a sour taste. Instead, eat more nutmeg, celery, banana, pineapple, papaya, and nutmeg. They don't only increase your taste down there; they increase your sexual prowess too. This is a foremost precaution you shouldn't forget. Remember your partner tends to linger longer if they enjoy every moment of it.

Good news, this is one of the sexual explorations that can never result in pregnancy.

Now, How Can You Have Oral Sex With A Female Partner?

It isn't enough to just tear right through her undies and lick the soft spot. That will be super boring don't you think?

- Flick the clitoris! It is always sensational when you flick the clits with your tongue. The touch of your tongue is softer on her clits. Remember it's got a natural lube, and it is super sensitive. Those things can spark electricity in every inch of her body, so, go for the clit!
- Penetrate: Did you assume penetration is meant for just the penis and some machines? Come on... The tongue can spice things than you can imagine! As long as it is fine by your partner. Dig the office as deep as you can, taunt and stroke till you catch that look on her face. There it is, you win! It doesn't matter whether she is pregnant or on her monthly flow, as long as it is fine by her, ride on with your lips.

So, What Are The Best Positions You Can Try With Her?

Flat Style
Often most times, it is pretty easier if you lie flat and allow your partner to do all the exploration himself. Simply lie on your back, with your legs straddle, of course. While he explores just a bit above you.

Flat Style 2
Pretty different and crazy. This time, it is his turn to lie flat on his back. His kneels should be edged at about 45 degrees. Kneel a bit above him and place the booty right above his mouth. He should use a pillow to prop his head if there is a need for it. In this position, you have unfettered access to taste the thighs beside the booty.

69
Ever heard about 69? A really hot style. You are both going to lie by your sides on the bed, by each other's sides. Do you know the freaking part? You are lying opposite each other! Your head is turned towards his toes and your toes, hers. Imagine what you both are opening to each other. It's just a grand way of licking each other at that same time. I can imagine that mountain of pleasure!

Get Her Comfortable

Receiving oral sex for men is easy not so for women. The position isn't exactly comfortable which is why it's important if you give her time to really get into position. Possibly the most comfortable position for oral sex would be lying down with pillows piled high under her pelvis. This tilts up the vagina and allows for a large opening, thereby giving you lots of room to work. In this position, guys also get lots of control and comfort so that they can play as much as they want.

Lick and Suck

Biting or nipping may be good for some guys receiving oral pleasure, but it's always a negative for the girls. Feel free to suck and lick as much as you want, but never let her feel the teeth because it will definitely bring her out of the moment.

Play with the Lips

The lips or labia is wonderfully sensitive, especially when it comes to light pressure. Using the edge of your tongue on this body part will definitely send a shiver down her spine, especially if you follow up with a good and long hard suck.

Locate the Clitoris

Know where the clitoris is located and have fun with it. Note, though, that the clitoris shouldn't receive all your attention. Remember that in this position, you have access to both the clitoris and the U-Spot, which is that sensitive plump flesh just a few centimes below the clitoris.

Listen and Learn

If you're not getting encouragement —either verbal or physical— you're probably not doing it right. Most women would moan or do something that tells you you're hitting the right spots. There are also instances when she'll grab the guy's hair and direct the movement of the lips and mouth, silently telling him where to go and which part to focus on. The tilting and shifting of the pelvis are also indicative of this particular need. Make sure to pay attention to these changes so you'll be able to fully give her the orgasm she wants or needs.

Not Just the Mouth

Note that oral sex isn't completely oral. In the same way, the women use their fingers when giving a blow job, men can also use their fingers during oral sex. In fact, it's usually a better idea since their fingers can enter and stretch the vagina in such a way that men can stimulate two important points all at once: the clitoris and the A-Spot. If men are particularly good, they can also hit the U-Spot and the K-Spot at the same time.

Best Oral Sex Tips

It mustn't be just oral sex

You can start off with oral sex and finish up with penetration. You can stop off with mild foreplay, penetrate, and finish off with oral sex. It doesn't have to be oral sex alone. Also, this doesn't mean it can't be orals sex alone.

You and your partner can have an orgasm from oral sex alone.

Don't stop after they cum

Even after your partner has had an orgasm, keep going for a short while.

Watch Porn

Watch porn together or let your partner alone watch porn while your head is buried in between their legs. This can be used to set the mood at the beginning or increase sexual tension while oral sex is still ongoing.

Talk Dirty

Before you go fully into oral sex, it is good to set the mood and create a more intense sexual tension by talking dirty to your partner. Tell them all the things you are going to do to them, whisper to them how hot their body is and how turned on you are by them. You can say something like, 'Oh baby, I can't wait to get a taste of your sweet juice, you'll eat you so hard, and you will forget your name. I'm so hard I can shoot a truckload of cum in your face,' It doesn't have to be these words exactly, but do you get my point?

Oral Sex Tips to Drive Her Crazy

To give a female a great orgasm, you will need to know the female body and all of the places that, when stimulated, will make a woman feel pleasure. Whether you are a female yourself or you are a male with a female partner, both sexes can benefit from learning more about the female body. We will look at the different pleasure centers in the female body, how to find them, and how best to stimulate them to lead to a mind-blowing orgasm.

The Clitoris

The clitoris is the place that most people think of when they think of the female orgasm. The clitoris is located very close to the vagina. It is a small bean-like structure that has many, many nerve endings located within it- which is why it can lead a female to reach orgasm. In terms of female pleasure centers, it is the most easily accessible, which is why it is the most well-known.

How to Find the Clitoris

To find the clitoris, begin by placing a hand on the pelvic area, with the fingers pointing downward (towards the vagina). A woman can do this for herself, or a man can do this to find his woman's clitoris. Whichever person is doing this will need to move their hand downward slowly, using their fingers to feel around. As they wrap their fingers underneath her pelvic region, approaching the vaginal region between her legs, they will need to begin feeling around for a small lump-like structure

The clitoris is said to be the female penis. This is because it enlarges and becomes engorged when a woman is sexually aroused. It will be easier to find a woman's clitoris if she is feeling aroused or horny. Only a small part of the clitoris is exposed to the outside of the body, but this is the reason why there are so many nerve endings located within it and the reason why stimulating it will lead to such intense pleasure. It is also the reason why it is easier to find when it is "erect."

How to Stimulate the Clitoris

Once you have found the clitoris, you will then be able to stimulate it to give yourself or your woman an orgasm. Begin by gently placing two fingers on it and putting a bit of pressure. Rub it by moving your fingers in small circles- making sure to be gentle. Continue to do this, and you/she should begin to become more aroused the more her clitoris is stimulated. By rubbing the clitoris, you will be able to stimulate the entire clitoris, even the part of it that you cannot see, and this will cause the woman to start to become wet inside of her vagina, which prepares her body for penetrative sex.

The Squeeze Move
Squeeze her external lips to surround the clit snugly; this makes the clit pop somewhat out of it. You would now be able to rub the vagina to the mons, one next to the other or around and around with your fingertips.

The Anchoring
Anchor two fingers, so you are between the inward and external lips on either side of the clitoris. Move the fingers into very small movements with the goal that the vibration is felt by the clitoris.

Party Time
For some ladies, because of additional nerve bundles in those zones, the two- or the ten-focus purposes of the clit can be entirely pleasurable. You may attempt to concentrate on these focuses on your stimulation and see if you get more answers.

The G-Spot

The G-Spot is a lesser-known spot than the clitoris, but a woman can have extreme amounts of pleasure if this spot is stimulated. The G-Spot can give a woman intense levels of pleasure because it is connected to the clitoris. Inside of a woman's body, where the clitoris extends inside of her, it meets the vagina. This spot where the clitoris meets the vagina is exactly where the G-Spot is located. This thin wall between the clitoris and the inside of the vagina allows for the pressure and stimulation that is being placed on the G-Spot to stimulate the deepest parts of the clitoris. Remember that the clitoris contains many nerve endings, and this is why the G-Spot can be so amazing for her- because there are even more nerve endings in the deeper parts of the clitoris.

How to Find the G-Spot

To find this spot, you will need to insert a finger into her vagina. It is best to try to find this spot after you have stimulated the clitoris for some time because, as I mentioned, then her vagina will have begun to lubricate itself to prepare for penetration. (Inserting a finger is still considered penetration). You can use this self-lubrication to your advantage, as it will make penetration more enjoyable for her because it will reduce any friction within the vagina and the vaginal area in general. When the vagina becomes very wet, it can lubricate the entire vaginal area (including the clitoris), which will then make it easier to stimulate using smooth motions as well—no friction results in smooth gliding motions, which results in pleasure and no pain.

When she is wet enough, slide a finger inside of her vagina while she is lying on her back (a woman can do this for herself too) and make a "come here" motion with your finger, so that you are moving your finger towards her belly button (the front of her body). Feel around in this area for a bumpy or rough surface. This textured area is the G-Spot. Just like the clitoris, the G-Spot is slightly different in every woman, but each woman's G-Spot will be located in the same general area, so this technique for finding it should work 99% of the time. The G-Spot will be of different sizes for different women, so be aware of this when trying to find it as well.

How to Stimulate the G-Spot

To give a woman pleasure by stimulating her G-Spot, you will need to place pressure on it over and over again, repeatedly, until she reaches orgasm. This can be done using your fingers, your penis, or sex toys of a variety of sorts.

Stimulating this spot with your fingers is quite simple as you will have lots of control, and you will be able to feel around to see if you are in the right spot. When you have found the G-Spot with your fingers, gently press on it with the pads of your fingers and avoid curling your fingers around too much as you don't want your nails to scratch the inside of her vagina. Press with the pads of your fingers on her G-Spot with light pressure, but enough for her to feel what you are doing. Continue to do this, and you should feel her vagina getting increasingly wetter. As you do this, you can increase the speed of stimulation if she wishes. Communicate with her to see what she wants you to do (faster, slower, harder, lighter, deeper, and shallower).

The penis can also stimulate the G-Spot, but it is a little harder to do as there will not be as much control as there is when using fingers. Try to choose a position that will have the curve of the penis line up with the front of the vaginal wall, and this will give you the best chance of hitting the G-Spot. We will go into this further later on in this book, where we will look at specific sex positions. For now, though, knowing where the G-Spot is located as well as how to find it and how to make a woman feel pleasure by stimulating that spot is a great start to being able to give her (or yourself) an amazing orgasm.

Work your way back. At the opening of the vagina, you should begin with your fingertips and make slow circles. Test different pressures and speeds with a great deal of input. At the opening, experience the rough, bumpy area, finally directly on the G-spot with slow circles.

Come here. The "coming here" movement, where, where your partner pulses one, two, or three fingers across the point, is the most effective G-spot movement. Numerous ladies like the trademark "Come Here" right above the bumpy area; others like it just underneath the pubic bone. You can bolt the fingers behind your pubic bone on the off chance that they are in the perfect spot.

Tap. Insert your partner's finger and tap the G-spot directly. You can proceed and walk gradually and perceive how much weight you can take. They can change the speed, as well.

The Anus

The anus is a very sensitive area for women, contrary to the beliefs of some people. While it is well-known that men have sensitive anuses and can receive pleasure here, a less well-known fact is that so can women! Women have very sensitive anal openings because there are many nerve endings here and a lot of surface area. This means that when stimulated, a woman can feel a lot of pleasure here. Because this is an area that rarely receives stimulation, when it does, it can be that much more enjoyable for a woman because she may not be used to the sensations.

The anus can also be stimulated with fingers, toys, or orally. Any of these ways can be enjoyable for the woman if she is open to receiving anal pleasure, as they will each give her a slightly different sensation. Think of how a warm tongue would feel vs. a smooth anal toy vs. the rough hands of the man she loves.

Blended Orgasms

A blended orgasm is achieved when multiple different orgasms are achieved at the same time. This can be two different orgasms at the same time, or in some cases, even more than two! This type of orgasm leads to even more pleasure than a single orgasm and will lead the woman to feel more intense pleasure than ever before. During penetration, there is lots of opportunity for different types of female orgasms to occur. The two most common ways that a woman can reach orgasm are through her clitoris and her G-spot. We will look at some ways that a woman can have both of these orgasms at the same time, as well as some other options for blended orgasms.

Any combination of these separate but simultaneous orgasms compounds to give the woman a mind-blowing, full-body, blended orgasm. Some of these zones include the clitoris, the anus, the G-Spot, and the nipples. Some women may have others as well, but this is largely dependent on the woman's body.

Oral Sex Tips to Drive Him Crazy

While male orgasms are usually straighter than female, you want to give your partner a variety of touches, including various strokes and pressure amounts. Enthusiasm, excitement, and imagination all make a difference between an average orgasm and an orgasm of Oh-My-God.

Some Myths about Men's Sexual Response

The first myth that stands in the way of good sex is that men should always be interested and sex-ready. There are numerous reasons why men don't always want to be sexual or why they develop sexual dysfunction. You can become exhausted and overworked, or you may feel fatigued after you start sex. They may also respond with feelings of distance or anger if they don't want to have sex or can't do it.

The second myth is that men will get hard as soon as sexual activity has started and will continue to be tough throughout their sexual experience. But after the adolescent hormonal peak (and occasionally even during this period, the capacity to maintain an erection fluctuates, depending on what kinds of sexual messages and experiences they have had). As men age, they need to stimulate themselves harder and harder on their cocks.

Erections that go up and down during one single sexual experience are the most physically healthy men who have not a functional reaction to dysfunctional conditions. Most men also frequently experience that an erection cannot be achieved. You can get performance anxiety if you believe that something is wrong with you if you do not get an erection, which makes the erection less likely to return. The more acknowledged and more not taken personally by your partners, the more likely you are to be able to benefit from the full erotic experience and the lower the chance of an ongoing erectile dysfunction.

As well as being under pressure to be hard, men (especially men who have sex with women) also experience a long-lasting pressure. As the average time, it takes men and women to orgasm is very different, women easily exert pressure to climax, and men put pressure on each other to last longer. There's no "right" time to have an orgasm, but the difference gives both men and women a lot of worry about performance. We worked with several people, and sometimes we're surprised at calls we receive to learn how to control their ejaculation. We asked one man who called in for orgasms with a question of self-described ejaculation control. He was relieved when he heard that the average time of men to last is seven minutes and that many females prefer a much more diverse sexual life and wouldn't wish to have a sex life for longer than that of their partner. "I usually come in about a one-half hour," he says, "but I want to please my partner completely."

The last harmful myth is that men should ejaculate in order. The fact is that a man has trouble climaxing sometimes, and that's normal. Some are much more likely to climax to certain sexual acts than others. At least some of the men will have to masturbate to ejaculate. When men feel that they are unable to orgasm or feel like the partner wants them to orgasm faster, one or both partners can go into "work mode." This is typically irritating, not attractive, and often triggers the orgasm to move away. The pressure on men to come on command or by specific sexual acts can be very helpful. Sex can be very pleasant for men whether they ejaculate, and it can be very hot to see a man coming to your body if he needs to give himself a helping hand.

Cocks

While most women want to warm-up well before their pussies are touched, as part of a warm-up, men may like the cock stroked or touched. When men want their cock to be touched, they should tell their partner. Some men feel very warm with touching the body of their partner, but it is also great to reciprocate and give your male partner all-round touch. Before you go down to his dick, you can touch him on his back, neck, chest, and stomach.

Unfortunately, most cocks are one-way touched. The men's partners take the handle, grasp it tightly, and float up and down their legs. While this can be awesome, cocks, like pussies, can be much higher if approached in a variety of ways. In the first place, you should, for example, run your fingers along the shaft and balls, kick the balls gently and taunt your fingertips on the head of the cock. To tease a soft dick can be as nice as a hard dick. Teasing is a great way to lure a pig into anticipation without the same pain. The more relaxed and exciting it is, the more you enjoy skin texture and gliding movement.

If you're with an uncircumcised person and you want to begin by putting your hand firmly on your head, use your hand to push the prepuce up and down. The prepuce is like an integrated lubrication system that hydrates and protects the cock's sensitive head. You may want to wear massage oils, cocoon oil, or lube if you're with a circumcised man or if you touch the head of a non-circumcised man's cock directly. Some kind of oil is usually better than cocks' lube, but don't use oil if you use condoms later because the condom will weaken and break down. You can always improvise by putting a spit on your hand if you have nothing around. Whether he is circumcised or not, the sensation can be improved when the skin of the cock is pulled down at its base. Squeezing the skin tightly on the body covers the surface of the nerve endings, so it's smoother.

The basic stroke is simply wrapping and pushing your hand up and down. You can play at various speeds and pressures. Generally, you would like to use lighter, slower strokes to anticipate and to move more and more rapidly to orgasm. The pressure levels and the most enjoyable touches vary greatly from one person to another. Women try to masturbate before their partners to show them how excited they are. Partners, pay attention to how women touch themselves if you watch them masturbate in front of you. The man may get stroke completely, rarely, or never across his head, up and down can the shaft, or he uses short strokes that mainly focus on the head. He may put a lot of pressure or very light strokes on his cock. See how he plays with himself and see if he affects himself, at least partly. This is probably the most effective stroke if you try to bring him to orgasm with your hand.

Advanced Cock Strokes

You can stroke a cock in several ways. Here are a few to check, but try to create your ideas too.

Tornado

Ensure your hand is lovely and wet or oily. Place your hand palm on your frenulum (section right underneath the head of the penis facing up when a man is sitting on the back, and his penis rests on his body) and wrap your fingers on top of your shaft and head of the cock and exercise a certain pressure. Now start turning your wrist around, so your fingers and palms are moving side by side over the cock.

Head Caresses

Use your fingertips with the wet or oily pads to glean across the head and tease like you coax and pull your head softly. Turn the head around your fingers.

Cock and Balls

Create a loop like the rubber strip and stretch the balls around the top of the scrotum. (Let your partner know how far you will pull to give the most pleasure.) Use the other hand to alternately do the simple stroke on the cock and fondle and tickle the balls. If you do this correctly, the skin around the balls will be tight, and you will have further access to the nerve endings.

Blow Jobs

As with the touch, a cock is usually sucked predictably: somebody puts it in his mouth directly, and his lips slide up and down. There is often a blow work approached like that, which must be done and quickly accomplished. Check-in and see what kinds of physiological and psychological stimulation you can get out of a blow job to make it feel fantastic and enjoyable. You may like your mouth's sensation or feeling strong because you can give it so much pleasure, and it is at your mercy. You can enjoy the sense you're used to. When men talk with us about blow jobs, we usually hear that if your partner enjoys the experience, blow jobs are much better.

As a woman with oral sex, an exciting, interesting blow job slowly begins and grows up. You can kiss his chest and thighs from your partner's lips. Take your time before you even get to the cock to make him realize that it's about to lick and suck his cock, but it's not enough. Start by kissing your dick or gliding your tongue across your head and shaft lightly. Kiss and also kiss the balls gently. Don't forget. You could also take his cock and roll it around your neck and touch your lips, cheeks, and even your leg. Pay special attention to the frenulum, as it is one of most men's most sensitive parts of the cock.

Use your hands to begin spinning and tapping balls as you start to lace the tip and coax it into your mouth. You can curl the skin on the shaft or circle and bring the balls down just like you did when you did a hand job. You do it now with your gentle rubbing, biting, and teasing of the dick. When you move your head up and down, your tongue can lick and flick over the shaft and frenulum. Use your hand to extend your mouth if your cock is large, and spit again to ensure that your hand or all your cock is moist.

Take a break from sucking your dick at some point and put your balls in the mouth. You can only fit one or both of them into your mouth, depending on their size. Turn around and suck it around your mouth. Women, try rubbing the balls to enjoy your partner a lot more. You can always use a hand to stimulate his cock while you lick and suck his ass.

If you want, your face can fuck him: hang on, and his cock moves in and out. A deep throat can also be tested. The easiest position to take a deep throat is 69 or 69 if you don't sit on his face but kneel along the side of his head. When you try this, make sure your mouth is not dry. For lubrication, you will need plenty of spit. Hold down, slowly open and relax your throat muscles, and let your partner slide. You may not be very far if you have a powerful gag reflex, but you can even let yourself gag a little and see if that is the turnaround for you.

If you spit or drink is up to you. As long as your partner has no sexually transmitted infection, the sperm are harmless, and if you just hold it in your mouth and wait for it to sprinkle, you may end up with a less bitter taste in your mouth. If you don't like the idea of having cum in your mouth, ask your partner to tell you when he is about to cum so you can finish it with your hand or let it go to a part of your body or towel. You can also use a blow job as a warm-up to a change in sex without him.

Achieving Orgasm

Reaching orgasm means a lot for women in intercourse. Let's not even talk about the fact that it reduces inflammation and cardiovascular risks. Orgasm provides relaxation and satisfaction. Remember, it is the point where a woman feels the top of the pleasure in lovemaking. A woman who reaches orgasm would feel whole at that moment. Her bones and her veins will feel weak as she goes numb in the lower parts of her body for a few minutes. She would feel happy, at ease, and she will feel delicate in a way she cannot explain.

According to Osmo Kontula, a famous sexologist, there are different ways a woman shows orgasm. Some would sob and hold their partner tighter than they had done earlier, for that fleeting moment. Many more experience orgasms but do not have any idea because they do not understand how complex anal or vaginal orgasm could be.

O'Reilly also records that most women expect themselves to scream loud and squirt all over during sex, as often seen in porn. But this is not necessary at all, except when the woman is the type who squirts originally. A woman will also find it super hard to climax if she doubts her sexual ability, feels bothered about a lot of things or remains uncomfortable during intercourse.

So, you should not keep pushing the intercourse towards the woman's orgasm. Rather, there are different levels of orgasm for a woman, and she wants you to take her through all of them. Reaching her orgasm should not be your priority; she wants you to give her all the pleasure at the different levels of intense sexual exploration. Even after orgasm, many women want you to caress and hold them as earlier. So, orgasm is just not everything.

The orgasm is the culmination of a sexual relationship, a climax that produces a pleasant feeling of a sudden release of accumulated tension from the moment when the excitement phase begins. It is at that moment that a series of intense muscle spasms are generated that are highly pleasing, which helps promote the release of endorphins that occur simultaneously.

Women experience orgasm in different ways, but usually, this is characterized by the fact that the acceleration of heart rate, breathing, and blood pressure reach their highest level and the vagina, uterus, anus, and muscles along with the pelvic bones contract between five and ten times at intervals of less than one second. However, some women may feel orgasm throughout their bodies and even get multiple orgasms.

The orgasm lasts only a few moments and then enters what is known as the resolution phase in which there is a general relaxation of the whole body, normalization of blood circulation and breathing, and with it a feeling of great placidity, tiredness, and even lethargy.

Many women confess not to reach it regularly and even never (anorgasmia). It is very important that the couple talks about it because experimentation and information can improve their sexual practice as well as learn to control ejaculation in the case of the man and enhance the excitement in the woman. Couple's therapy can be a good option to solve this sexual dysfunction.

The Female Orgasm

Contractions start at 0.8-second intervals, and their number can vary greatly, decreasing after intensity, duration, and frequency. More than a localized response in the pelvis, it is a total response of the organism. Imagination is directly related to orgasm; the brain has a lot to do with it. With the penetration, the entire vulvar pyramid is mobilized synchronously and the G-spot and the clitoris are stimulated. Every woman has the physical ability to experience orgasms.

These are the symptoms of female orgasm:

- Greater increase in heart rate.
- Increase in breathing.
- Increase in blood pressure.
- The subjective sensation of the explosion of pleasure.
- Contraction of the uterus.

Contraction of the Orgasmic Platform

After the orgasm, there is a recovery in the woman prior to the excitement. Although if she is re-stimulated before the sexual tension decreases, the woman can experience several successive orgasms.

The Female Orgasm: Keys to Reach It

The female orgasm is not only achieved through penetration. It is highly recommended to explore the female body to discover erogenous zones that facilitate the task. In the case of sexual intercourse, foreplay, oral sex, and other pleasurable practices can be the perfect vehicle to achieve an unforgettable orgasm. Meanwhile, it is also essential:

- That your partner knows how their body "works" so they can be better at "playing" and experiencing things with you, and to know oneself through self-exploration. So, if you want to enjoy your body and your pleasure areas, try one of these useful toys.

1. **Physical Manifestations of Female Orgasm**

During Orgasm:

- The clitoris retracts,
- The vagina, the perineum, and the uterus contract due to shaking
- The nipples harden.
- The heart accelerates.
- The blood vessels dilate.

Everything is stimulated during this supreme pleasure with which women (and men, in their case) go mad. And it is normal because the orgasm involves the secretion of endorphins, the molecule of happiness, which provides a feeling of unequaled well-being.

2. **How to Achieve a Female Orgasm**

In general, most women achieve orgasm when they stimulate sexual areas alone or in pairs:

- Preliminary caresses: Activate your brain by preparing for the moment of intercourse. These movements increase the pleasure much more and help you reach orgasm faster.
- Cunnilingus: One of the techniques that are very exciting for some women, and that will help if they suffer from anorgasmia and have trouble reaching orgasm.
- Masturbation: Whether you do it yourself or your partner, it will get the genital area excited more easily.
- Penetration: Through penetration of the penis, a woman may also reach orgasm. It is one of the most essential parts that lead us to intercourse, to the female orgasm, and also to the ejaculation of a man.

But the best way to reach orgasm is knowing your own body. We have different erogenous points that can make us feel in the seventh heaven, but you have to find them!

The Solution: Start in the Discovery of The Body:

- Alone or as a couple,
- With sexual toys or without them, to detect the most moving areas.

3. **Different female orgasms**

Vaginal orgasm: Achieved by stimulation of the Gräfenberg point or more commonly called "G-spot," located about 4 cm from the entrance of the vagina. It has a ball shape of less than one centimeter and increases in size with stimulation. It is located beside the bladder, so it is not strange that after female vaginal orgasm, we feel like going to the bathroom. To sensitize, stimulate it regularly with gentle and repeated pressures with the point of the finger or with the help of a sex toy. Try these toys if you want to get an incredible vaginal orgasm:

- Massager vibrator with 30 different modes.
- Chinese vibrating silicone balls with remote control.
- Vibrator with heat effect for women.

Clitoral orgasm: This is achieved by stimulation of the clitoris. That is a small button located between the lips, anterior to the vagina. It can be accessed very easily. It is very sensitive. You can reach orgasm with delicate caresses. Here we leave you a few positions that will facilitate the pleasant task. These are the best sex toys to stimulate the clitoris:

- Satisfier Pro, clitoral sniffer.
- Clitoral massager with cunnilingus effect.
- Vibrator clitoris massager.

4. The Female Orgasm

Clitoral orgasm: According to a study 95% of women achieve orgasm through masturbation, and less than half, 45% achieve it with penetration of the male penis.

The vaginal orgasm: There are few women who manage to reach this type of orgasm. Only 30% have the joy of experiencing such pleasure. Although all women have a G-spot, they have to get "woken up" with multiple movements in this area. For this, there are positions that favor it: the missionary, with the legs of the woman on the back of the man or the greyhound, with which a deep penetration is facilitated.

5. Female Multi-Orgasm Is Possible

Although for some it is only a fantasy, the truth is that multi-orgasm exists and is easier to achieve than it seems. The key is in:

- Know your own body,
- Know what is possible
- Put your mind on it,
- Lengthen the sexual climax (many times we do not achieve it because our partner lasts less than we would like),
- Change up stimuli and erogenous zones.
- Choose positions that really work with us.

Men's Orgasm

Orgasm for Men, What Do They Want?

The same way orgasm is the climax of it all for women; men peak their pleasure in inexplicable ways when they reach orgasm. Unlike a woman's orgasm; however, a man's orgasm is direct and visible. It results in ejaculation.

Like women, a man does not begin lovemaking with his mindset on reaching orgasm. Instead, he focuses on having pleasure. He concentrates on enjoying every moment with the partner and maximizing the sexual exploration of his partner. As Robert Hamilton reports in SEXUAL AWARENESS, most men hate to reach an orgasm before reaching a strong, fulfilling sexual experience. They are dedicated to increasing the period of lovemaking and the delight of their partner before reaching their orgasm. Quebec University conducted research to assess the effect of women's orgasm on women. It was discovered that up to 65% of respondents felt that getting their partner to climax made them felt better as accomplished men. Women recognize this, and so, fake orgasm many times.

Rather than a fake orgasm, a woman can help his partner to improve the period before his orgasm and sexual exploration by doing the following:

1. Guide him. Show him the erogenous parts of your body and guide him to explore them.
2. Get his mindset on the exploration. Flirt with him and turn him on. Whisper sensational things about his strength, how much you love, and how much you want him to have you. Continue to whisper pouring words on him as you make love with each other.
3. Change sexual positions. Adjusting can help a man last longer.
4. Try to help him relax and focus as much as possible.
5. Spark his head before sex. If you had plans to have sex at night. Spark his head all through the day. Flash him a sexy or half-nude picture. Show him a sensational part of you that he finds irresistible and ensure he takes diets that can increase his time in bed.

Women and men want the same things in sex; pleasure, intimacy, and love. Achieving orgasm should not be the priority of either party, and men would have more fun if they didn't feel the obligation to be in control of sexual exploration every time. Unwind and have fun, forget orgasm, and explore each other!

What Does He Want?

For males, once the blood flow and heart rate have increased, their genitals will grow in length and become firm (similar to the female reaction). As the sexual activity continues (be it foreplay or intercourse), the genital muscles go through a series of contractions, tensing and releasing as reproductive fluids are pushed into the urethra to be ejected once the male reaches his climax and peaks. Men have less difficulty inspiring and achieving release, but their orgasms tend to be shorter (an issue that can easily be overcome through building sexual endurance).

Best Sex Positions for Male Orgasm

Cowgirl

Make him rests on his back, mount yourself over him with every leg on either side of his middle. Instead of bouncing all over, you can concentrate more on moving your crotch to and fro, scouring your clitoris on his open and paunch district. You can likewise pound your pelvis around and around while kneeling. It causes you to spread your legs more extensively. Keep your hand laid on his chest, causing him to sit in a semi-inclined position where his back is leaned against the casing of the bed.

Being on top gives the lady unlimited authority with respect to the speed, pace, profundity, and movements. Men additionally last longer as this position is easy for them, and they simply can sit and appreciate, snacking at your areolas, kissing your neck and lips, squeezing your bosoms, and crushing your body.

Face Off

This position involves the man sitting on the edge of the bed so that the lady can be on top and take control. It is similar to the sensual pose "The Amazon," but allows for the lady to get more leverage so she can gain deeper penetration and greater speed.

Him: You want to sit on the edge of the bed with your feet planted firmly on the floor. This won't work on a chair but may work on another surface like a counter or the couch. When she mounts you, you can hold her bum for added control, or you can simply wrap your hands behind her and let her control the movements.

Her: You are going to mount your man and keep your knees on either side of his hips. You want to keep your shins down on the surface, and your toes curled under so that you can have maximum control over movements. This will give you the opportunity to control the depth of penetration and speed of movements. You can wrap your hands behind his shoulders to help with added support and momentum.

Leap Frog

This is similar to a doggy style pose but allows for deeper penetration and greater pleasure for both. It is a man-in-control pose, but the woman can add some effort into the movements as well. Because of the female's position, she can also use her own hands to stimulate her clitoris during penetration.

Her: You are going to prop yourself up on your knees and then fold over so that your chest is on the bed. With your free hands, you can play with yourself or simply get comfortable and relax into the experience.

Him: You are going to enter your girl from behind just like it is doggy style. You should be on your knees to gain entry, and you can use your hands on her hips to help you get leverage to penetrate more effectively.

Women's Orgasm

Tantric sex, in particular, will help with a woman's orgasm. There is a big difference between the ordinary orgasm that you get from sex and tantric orgasms, and oftentimes, it will change how the woman feels.

Many times, these can last for hours, and in women, this can change their sexual health. There is a command during a tantric orgasm that reaches your brains' control center, and hat's through the hypothalamus and the pituitary gland, and I will majorly benefit the sex life of women in particular.

A lot of the hormone oxytocin gets released during a tantric orgasm, and this alone can boost your mood, the position you feel in life, your passion, your emotion, and your social skills. Having tantric sex can do all of this, and I can benefit you in your daily activities.

It'll Make You More Patient

Tantric sex isn't just for sexual pleasure; it helps with developing life skills and building on weaknesses.

Do you sometimes kind of just want to get it done rather than go through the deep connection w=in the moment? You might not even realize it because your body and mind are fueled by hormones, but tantric sex promotes patience, which is something of a virtue that everyone can have during sex. However, this can also help you to build a deeper, better connection with your partner.

Sometimes, tantric sex is a little bit awkward since many people aren't used to just sitting there, focusing on their partner, breathing together, and developing a real look at the person they're with. Some people don't even realize they do this either.

Do you tend to have sex with either your eyes closed or the lights off? While dimming the lights aids to the ambiance, tantric sex makes it a little different. Tantric sex is actually a meditative process, and they encourage you to hold back the orgasm. It didn't denial; it's your conscious effort to hold it back so you and your partner can have a conscious moment together.

Patience develops naturally from this. You might not even realize it, but you learn to understand and appreciate your partner a whole lot more after engaging in tantric sex. Those things that used to piss you off every now and then? Well now, if you practice tantric sex, this patience develops, and you grow stranger with your partner over time.

Helps with Problem Solving

This might seem a bit strange, but for those starting, it's a different type of activity that you might not be used to. Those who are beginners or new to the experience might realize that the positions required for tantric sex are much more varied than just the same old positions.

Some of them might not even provide much pleasure to you either.

This requires you to work together with your partner. It has sex a team activity, where both of you need to talk it out and work together as well, in order to enjoy pleasure.

This can oftentimes be embarrassing because both of you are vulnerable in this state, but it helps with problem-solving skills and builds that connection. Plus, if you're a team, you'll have a much stronger connection outside of the bedroom, and work to solve the problems you have going on outside of the bedroom as well.

This also stimulates creativity. That's because we're embracing the concept of "supra sexuality" which expresses our purpose which is creativity and empowerment in order to unlock our full potential. Sex might be used to create human life of course, but it also brings forth new and creative actions that will help you experience a pleasurable sensation in order to achieve the goals that you have during intercourse as well.

Let's You Be Selfless

Do you sometimes feel like your partner is a little selfish in the bedroom? Do you sometimes feel you might be a tiny bit selfish? It might be because of the fact that you're not withholding your orgasm.

There is a benefit to doing this, and that's something to mention. Oftentimes, people don't realize that tantric sex offers the power of liberation, which allows for you to have an amazing experience that is often compared to glimpsing into the cosmic consciousness of the other person, fostering a deeper, more responsible understanding of the person.

Oftentimes, some people don't realize how selfish they are until they have the tantric orgasm, which will change their life and blow their minds. Oftentimes, they might not even realize that they are like this until it happens.

But for the other person, it can benefit them too. Sex is a two-person activity, and if you and your partner are both not talking out what will benefit the other person, and your partner isn't a little bit selfless, it can cause problems later on. You need to walk into this with the idea of supporting one another into orgasms since this will help others remember and get a better idea of giving rather than just receiving.

We're a culture focused on the receiving end of sex. While it's fun, also giving to the other person can have some marked benefit to you as well.

Creates More Empowerment

Finally, it'll make you feel empowered.

What does empowerment actually mean? It's more than just mere power. Power is something that most people confuse empowerment with, but they're very different.

The organic sexual pleasure that you get from tantric sex strips away the pretenses and helps check your ego. Empowerment is what comes after you check your ego and experience the wild nuances of tantric sex. It oftentimes brings about that vulnerability, stripping away all of the other stuff that you might've hidden or been ashamed of giving you a sense of purpose and the ability to express your fears and loves on a deeper level.

For those of us who have trouble being this vulnerable, this can be scary. I get that, but understand that, with the right mindset and the right understanding of the fact that you're in this for the long haul, and you'll experience pure, unadulterated pleasure, is something amazing.

You'll realize over time that you're stronger, and you can tackle more of life. People who experience tantric sex have power, but it isn't a power that they use for bad or a power that they don't know how to wield. Now, it's their own sense of power they've learned from experiencing this, which is mind-blowing.

People don't realize how this changes you, how having tantric sex will blow your mind, but also strip you of all of the facades you've put up about sex. The idea of hiding under the sheets, turning the lights off, not looking at your partner, all of that gets fully stripped away through tantric sex.

Tips and Tricks (How to last Longer)

The Pause-Squeeze Method

The "pause-squeeze" is one of the techniques for preventing an early climax. When you're about to ejaculate, tell your partner so that she can squeeze the end of your penis. It is a point where the head of your penis is joining the shaft. She should squeeze the point for several seconds, till your urge to climax passes. You should be waiting for another 30 seconds before restarting your strokes and foreplay. She can reduce the sensation of tightness inside her vagina by relaxing the internal muscle and opening the thighs generously.

There are other spots to be squeezed, such as the base of the shaft, the underside of the head that is packed with sensitive nerves, and spots between the base of the scrotum and the anus (the swollen path carrying urine as well as the semen). By squeezing these spots, the climax can be delayed.

Hand Job

Some couples say that they last longer if they masturbate together before a lovemaking session. This desensitizes the penis and the vagina to some extent. Women can have oral sex and use sex toys alternately to enable them to have an orgasm. Most women admit that they have better chances of an orgasm when they use sex toys for stimulation, though they like the stimulation through the tip of the tongue from their lover on a regular basis. Oral sex is used by women to stimulate men and to communicate heartfelt love and intimacy.

Delay Penetration

If you delay penetration by spending more time in different types of foreplay and oral sex and allow her to reach her climax first, you can have prolonged lovemaking and you can climax together when she has a second climax. It takes 20 minutes for a woman to climax, whereas men last for nearly 2 to 5 minutes after they penetrate.

Counseling

Counseling sessions can help you reduce performance anxiety, feeling of guilt, and psychologically boost your confidence. If you are lasting for less than 3 minutes, you may require expert medical advice.

Lifestyle Changes and Herbal Solutions

Balance your diet with additional nutrients with a variety of fruits and vegetables. Bananas, Indian gooseberry (Alma), beetroot, and strawberries are some of the foods you may want to add to your diet.

A popular fruit to prevent early ejaculation has been blueberries. They are packed with nutrients that relax the pelvic blood vessels, thus improving the blood flow to your penis. This helps you to last longer. Consuming blueberries on a regular basis can cure premature ejaculation as they contain dopamine, which is the "feel-good" hormone, which can regulate the flow of semen during the onset of the climax.

Other herbal remedies for a better sex life include:

1. Nutmeg (Jaiphal)
2. Asparagus adsendens
3. Gokshura (Tribulus Terrestris)
4. Garlic
5. Shilajit
6. Ashva gandha or Indian ginseng for male rejuvenation
7. Shatavari or asparagus racemousus (for females)

You should reduce alcohol and avoid smoking. Quitting these may be difficult, but it may boost your chances of lasting longer on a long-term basis.

Yoga postures such as Bhujangasan (cobra pose) and Paschimotthanasana help the flow of oxygen and blood to the genitals, enhancing the ability to last longer. Strengthen the abdominal muscles by yoga and Pranayama. Practice deep breathing every day on an empty stomach for ten minutes. Pelvic exercises help you control erections and sustain them over a long period.

Practice Squeeze Stop While Urinating

While urinating, use a squeeze stop and release technique. Use fifteen interruptions, each of ten seconds, while you urinate for several seconds in between. This should be practiced three times a day.

By interrupting urine flow, you will be exercising your pubococcygeus muscle (PC muscle). These muscles are located all over from the urinary sphincter to the anus. They're the ones that stretch from the anus to the urinary sphincter. By squeezing your PC muscle, you improve blood flow to your penis and train yourself on how to delay ejaculation when you are extremely aroused.

Use of Medicated Condoms and Other Tips

The top part of the penis, the head, in particular, is highly sensitive, and stimulation on this part can be reduced by the use of condoms. Changing the angle of strokes and grinding of the hips in a too and fro movement can reduce the sensation, thus helping you stay on.

Lidocaine is a medicine injected by the dentist to reduce the pain of the gums of patients. Condoms lined with this drug Lidocaine are now available, but they need a doctor's prescription. On the other hand, a higher dosage of Lidocaine on the layer of the condom's inner surface may not allow the initial erection at all.

If you plunge deep inside of your women's vagina and stay there while she has relaxed thighs, the sensation can reduce on the head of the penis.

When early ejaculation is occasional, the root cause could be psychological. Men who feel guilty or have the fear of getting caught could ejaculate even before they penetrate.

Men may not last longer during the initial few maiden adventures. It should not bother them. Having sex with the right females in the right comfort settings, with minimum outside stresses could enhance their regular sexual performance.

Before the climax begins, during intercourse, some groups of nerves called Krause finger corpuscles send some signals from the penis to control centers in the brain that control semen flow and ejaculation. If dopamine levels are high in blood flow due to the feeling of guilt or fear, control centers in the brain send an urgent signal to the muscles in the penis to throw semen out quickly. Keeping the mind under control is important to reduce guilt and fear. This can be done by adopting yoga and meditation.

Postures with women on top or alternating between men on top and woman on top after initial penetration can enable the male partner to keep his penis erect for a longer period of time. Changing postures from the rear penetration position to the woman on top position can help women to last longer.

Experts also suggest the "7 and 9" technique, which means 7 super-fast in and out thrusts followed by 9 slow in and out strokes. You should also use a combination of deep thrusts and shallow thrusts, as well as hip rotations.

How Can Sex Toys Improve Your Sex Life?

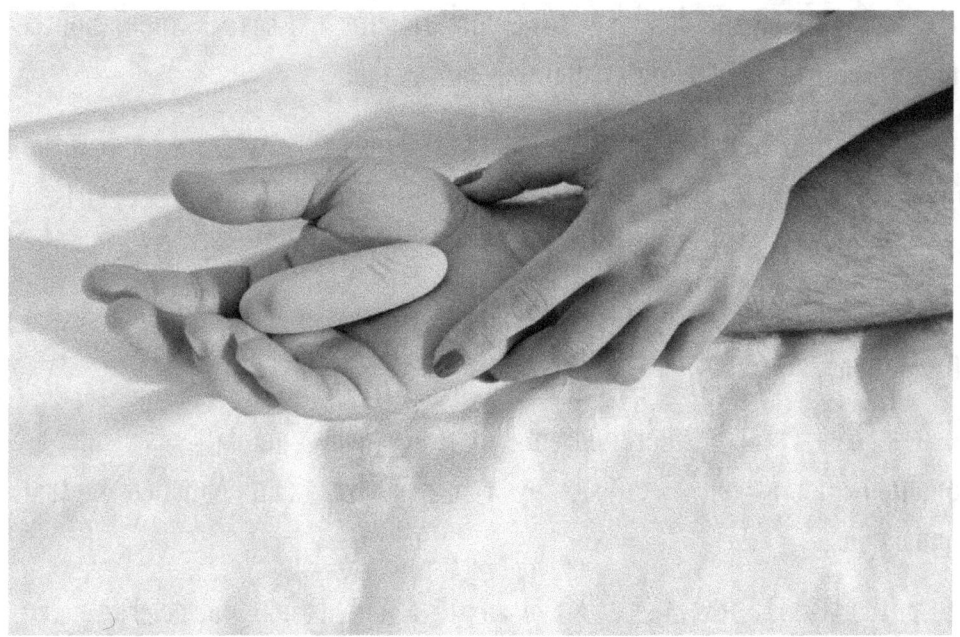

Some people view sex toys as something that is for those who have wild kinks or those who cannot perform without the assistance of some sort. In reality, though, sex toys are designed to increase and enhance pleasure for anyone. By using sex toys, you do not have to engage in anything wild or anything that you are uncomfortable with. You are also not admitting that you have a sexual problem by using a sex toy.

One of the ways in which sex toys can improve your sex life is that they allow you to focus on one area of the body while the sex toy takes care of pleasure in another. For example, a sex toy that is designed to pleasure a woman's clitoris will do so while you can focus on her nipples or her vagina.

Enhances Body Knowledge- The use of sex toys during sex helps partners explore each other bodies and understand the part with more sensory stimulation.

Enhances Sexual Pleasure- The combination of these toys with sex provides additional pleasure.

Self Confidence- While using sex toys, you are sure that sexual stimulation is guaranteed making you aim at attaining satisfaction.

Quick Orgasm- The hyper intensive stimulation caused by sex toys reduces the time a partner would require to attain an orgasm. For that reason, sex starts at the right time with little effort applied.

Control Sexual Needs- Sex toys could be used by either partner for sexual stimulation.

Fosters Love- The exploration of your partner's genitals as well as communication as you try out sex toys removes barriers and enhances mutual connections.

Prevents STIs- The use of sex toys means that genitals may not need to make contact thus preventing the spread of sexually transmitted Infections.

Improves Performance- The sensitivity associated with sex toys boosts the partner's morale, making them perform above par.

Prevents Unwanted Pregnancy- The fact that sex toys do not ejaculate makes it safe for the woman from impregnation.

Best Sex Toys for Beginners

The Vibrator

A vibrator is probably the most common sex toy available for female pleasure. Vibrators are the best choice for women who are new to sex toys and are unsure of what they may be looking for. A vibrator is a nice and easy place to start, and it can be used in a variety of ways. They can be used by a woman alone during masturbation, by a woman with a partner. They can be used during penetration and during foreplay. Vibrators are such a versatile sex toy as they come in so many different shapes, sizes, and materials.

The Dildo

A dildo is a penis-like object that provides pleasure by being inserted into the vagina or the anus, and that works in much the same way as a penis does. Dildos can be made of a variety of different materials such as glass, stainless steel, or silicone, and they come in a wide variety of colors and shapes from realistic-looking penises to pink and purple banana-shaped ones. The world of dildos is vast and encompasses any kind of penetrative device you could possibly dream of.

Dildos can be used by a woman or a man on their own while masturbating or with a partner. A woman can use a dildo by inserting it into her vagina to stimulate her G-Spot and a man can use it to stimulate his prostate during masturbation. Dildos can be used with a partner, as well. Your partner can use a dildo on you by inserting it into the vagina or the anus in order to please you. Most dildos can be taken into the bathtub or shower as well, so you can have shower sex with it if you wish. A dildo can be used in the vagina or the anus, whichever you prefer, and you can use the same dildo for both of these places, so you don't need to buy two.

Things to Know About Using Sex Toys

Sex toys are becoming popular, especially among the youth and couples. While there are different types of sex toys, some could be exciting and others intimidating. It would be very tricky trying out a toy that you have never used before. For that reason, you should make the following considerations to get the best toy for you and maximize enjoyment and pleasure.

- Start easy—When selecting your first sex toy, you should start with the simplest toys there are. This way, you can work up to more advanced toys in the future. Start steadily to avoid disappointments and intimidations.
- Cleanliness—It is essential to keep your body clean and hygienic, especially your genitals. Therefore, ensure you select sex toys that are cleaned easily and less likely to attract bacteria while in storage.
- Preference—It is common to find that what works for the service provider is not what will work for you. For that reason, you should ensure you acquire a sex toy depending on your likes and preference.
- Research—Finding reviewed products online has become simpler; hence, the importance of understanding a sex toy before purchasing or trying it.
- Storage—Extra care is needed when storing sex toys. They could react to materials placed near them. It is common to find silicone or latex toys looking melted.
- Consult with your partner—It is for your good to be upfront, open, and honest to your partner about the desires you have with sex toys. Similarly, let them know your preference and use their reaction to judge whether they are okay with it.

- Maintain Communication—It is the most crucial part of sex, especially when using sex toys. This way, your partner lets you know the part that is stimulated by the toy making it possible to discover additional erogenous zones.
- Maintain Safety—It is advisable to use these toys for the sole purpose for which they are meant. You should be cautious when using these toys for good sex. Notably, problems occur whenever users fail to follow instructions.

Lubricants

Using lube alone is not enough. You need to consider the type of lube if you want to create some magic between the sheets. Some lubes can cause allergic reactions or irritations if you're not careful, and there is nothing worse than feeling like that burning sensation on your penis or vagina.

Water-Based

These are the most versatile out of all the lubes and safe for all sexual activities. They are even safe to use on sex toys, making water-based lubes are the most popular choice. They're inexpensive, easily available, doesn't stain, and is safe to ingest in small amounts during sex (read the list of ingredients first though). Don't worry if you're using diaphragms or latex condoms. They're safe to be used on these products too. Water-based lubes are the popular choice among women because it feels like natural vaginal lubrication. Plus, they are incredibly easy to wash off once you're done, leaving your skin clean and residue-free.

Oil-Based

For a long-lasting, smooth, and silky experience, oil-based lubricants are a good choice to consider. Since they are thicker and creamier, they last longer during sex too. If you're masturbating, oil-based lubricants can be a great choice, but be cautious with these since not all oil-based lubes are safe to use when there are latex contraceptives involved. Oil-based lubes can be combined with water-based lubes during sex.

Silicone-Based

These last a very long time and a great if you're planning to get frisky in the water. They are also safe to use on latex condoms, but the downside is that it's not the best idea to use them on silicone sex toys since they will damage the surface area of the toys.

Petroleum-Based

These you want to stay well away from if you can since they are difficult to wash off and could cause some irritation by altering the vagina's pH levels. This could potentially lead to yeast infection, and plus, they destroy any latex-based products that you might be thinking about using them on. Not a great idea.

How to Boost Your Sexual Performance

Sexual Mindset At some point in your relationship, sex with your partner may become boring or a routine that you just have to follow. If you are currently stuck in a sexual rut with your partner, you are not alone, and most couples experience this. If you are stuck in a boring sex routine with your partner, you have got to push the reset button. That is, you have got to bring back the spark in your sex life. According to sex experts, familiarity is the death of sex drive. This is to say that the more you get used to your partner, the less exciting sex becomes. When that happens, you don't have to give up or leave your partner for someone else.

Liberate Your Body's Energy in A Different Way

Try something new to liberate your body's energy. You can join a dancing class or try yoga. Once you reignite your connection with your body, doing that with your partner won't be difficult. A recent survey found that sexually inactive partners felt unattractive to them and also experience feelings of sadness. Reignite the spark in your sex life by trying different ways to move and get comfortable in your body.

Create Time to Learn More About Sex

It could be at night. Take one night with your partner to have an uncensored discussion about sex. Talk about what you like and don't like sexually, talk about the hidden fantasies you have, and try new sex positions. If you and your partner have always been doing the missionary sex position, chances are your sex life will become boring. So, spice it up by trying new positions. While at it, don't put yourself under pressure; just experiment with sex positions and see what you like. If there are some fantasies you have, and you kept quiet about it out of fear of sounding insensitive, tell your partner "this night." Research shows that men and women have different sexual expectations, and these expectations do not just change overnight. As such, it's important for partners to discuss their likes and dislikes to have a pleasurable experience in bed.

Reignite Your Dopamine with a Fresh Experience

Trying something new with your partner promotes bonding and intimacy. Consider activities that might excite you or scare you, and it could be an escape Room or an amusement park ride. Doing these activities with your partner helps to create dopamine, and in the process, you get to experience the love and feelings you had when you started the relationship. According to health experts, the brain secretes dopamine and other chemicals, which promotes romantic passion and physical attraction. When you try a new activity with your partner, your brain secretes dopamine, and that helps to spark arousal.

Go On a Sexy Overnight Getaway, If You Are Up For It

Go on a sexy overnight getaway with your partner with role play. Decide beforehand the characters you will play dress up and enjoy the time with your partner. According to the U.S Travel Association, couples who go on trips together have better sex lives.

For some couples who are finding it hard to reignite the spark in their sex life, going on a sexy overnight getaway might put too much pressure on them. A better alternative is to spend time together trying nonsexual activities. You can visit a new local spot that just opened around the corner together or go hiking together.

Pleasure Yourself In Front of Your Partner

When you masturbate in front of your partner, they get to see how you enjoy pleasure, and that promotes intimacy. Allowing your partner to see how you like to be touched and where you like to be touched means you are making yourself vulnerable, and that builds intimacy and closeness. Masturbation benefits the body in a number of ways, and that includes relieving built-up stress, improving our mood, and that is a precursor for more sex.

If you and your partner like adventure, wear a remote-control sex toy in front of your partner and let him hold the remote control. This serves as a form of foreplay to get you excited before the main game.

Take a Sex Class and Practice on Weekends

Take a sex class with your partner. Finding a sex class is as easy as setting up a Facebook account. At the set class, you can learn new sex techniques, positions, props, and toys for sex play in a fun learning environment. Don't just learn alone; practice the things you have learned. While at it, don't put yourself or your partner under pressure; take it slow and gradually bring back the spark in your sex life. If you are looking to improve your sexual life and transform your relationship, taking a sex class is a great suggestion.

Have a One-To-One Talk with Your Partner to Air Out Seeded Stress

Communication is extremely important in a relationship, and lack of communication often contributes to dry spells in a relationship. A recent survey found that partners who argue and resolve the conflict were 10 times happier than those who covered the conflict. So, if you avoid conflict with your partner rather than talk about it and resolve it, your sex life is heading to the rocks. You'll be shocked that having hard conversations with an hour partner helps to build intimacy. Don't take offense or be discovered by what your partner says; instead, your goal should be taking measures to improve your relationship. The truth is identifying what's wrong in your relationship will help to improve it. Even if you and your partner do not have the same sexual energy, talk about it, and think of creative ways to fix the inequity.

Get Cozy and Chill with an Erotic Movie

There are a lot of porn clips on the Internet that are couple friendly. For adventurous and wild couples, sex experts advise attending a weekend sex convention. In the city you live in, sex conventions are organized year-round.

At the sex convention, you get to attend sex classes and even watch sex play. Learn one or two things and try them when you get home.

If switching up sex positions and techniques and trying the tips discussed doesn't work, you might have to tap into your inner needs. Most people aren't aware that stress and our daily activities greatly affect sexual intimacy. So, what you need might just be to tap into your inner needs to get back on track. Do not allow embarrassment or fear stops you from trying new things with your partner. This new technique might make you reach climax and enjoy ecstasy that you haven't enjoyed before. Sex with your partner can feel new and sweet. You just need to push the reset button.

Advanced Tips

Sex is a composition of various movements, erogenous zones, techniques, and sensations, so be assured that there are always ways to make things more amazing in the bedroom. Here are some advanced tips that can help guys and girls get the most out of each coupling.

Take Your Time

The common issue for most men with sex is that they take things too fast, failing to provide women with sufficient time to really get things in gear. Hence, she's not properly aroused and therefore unlikely to reach orgasm.

Give proper attention to the prelude or the foreplay, not just through the stimulation of the erogenous zones but also by making her comfortable and mentally ready. It is often said that the biggest and most powerful erogenous zone is the brain — which is why the Kama Sutra extensively talks about courtship and how to make the woman receptive to the advances of the male.

The Use of Sounds

Moans and other sounds coming from the female are highly arousing for many males and show that the female is leisurely enjoying the situation. Hence, females who want to increase the satisfaction for their male partners should be vocal about the sensations they are feeling and the pleasure of the sexual act. Additional caresses, pinching, sucking, and licking aren't exclusively done by males. Women will find that performing additional tasks during sex, particularly to the erogenous zones of the male will enhance his satisfaction.

It has also been proven that men are very visual when it comes to sex. Hence, a large number of them enjoy watching the female pleasure herself during sex, either by touching her breasts or playing with the clitoris.

Alternate

The Kama Sutra talks about the need to change pace, actions, and intensity during the sexual act. The fact is that there is no specific formula for the perfect sex. Different people have different methods of enjoying the act and may require different methods for stimulation. While others are perfectly happy with the typical foreplay, others may like it better to have their lovers wearing leather or performing some service. The same is true with kissing, touching, licking, biting, and other actions. Alternating from soft to hard, fast to slow, and then vice versa can keep the passion and pleasure going, ensuring both parties remain in the throes of sexual intensity.

You'll find that there's also no specified time length for sex. While women generally need lots of foreplay, there are situations when she is quickly and properly aroused so that there's nothing left to do but penetrate and thrust. Other times, you'd like it slow and lingering so that both parties can truly enjoy the moment. The differences and the failure to predict how sex will occur is part of the excitement.

Talk About It

Talking about sex —whether before or after— is usually a good idea. For some couples, the conversation is done during sex. We're not talking about the 'emotional' stuff here but rather a talk about what gets you satisfied and what doesn't. This is important because although observing the reaction of your lover is a good starting point; it doesn't always provide a clear picture of how satisfactory sex life happens to be.

Couples are encouraged to talk about what gets them off and what sexual acts they do NOT like in the bedroom. Only through this can you perfect the sex and really get satisfaction into the bargain. Remember: every person is different, so you'll have to adjust your actions depending on the person you're with.

Mirrors, Videos, and Locations

You can also further boost sexual pleasure by strategically placing mirrors in different parts of the bedroom or house so that you can watch yourself having sex. This is a big turn on for guys and actually provides a whole new dimension to the sexual union. The recording of the sex can also be terribly exciting, although, of course, you'll have to take careful steps to ensure that no one else views the act, especially if you have no intention of becoming a porn star.

Choosing different locations in the house to have sex in also kicks up the excitement a notch. For the most part, different locations in the house make it possible for couples to be inventive with sexual positioning. For example, wall sex is best done in the shower, while table sex can be done in the dining room. At the very least, sex in different locations of the house gives couples the chance to embed a memory into the specific location, allowing them to have something pleasant to remember each time they use the facilities.

Tips for Better Male Pleasure

The Closed Door

This position is similar to the missionary in that both people are lying down face-to-face, and the man is on top. The difference, however and what makes this an advanced position is that the woman will keep her legs shut the entire time tightly. The man's penis can be inserted while her legs are open, and then once it is in, she will close her legs. What this does is constrict her vagina and make the canal tighter for the man's penis. In addition to this, if she is aroused, her vagina will be engorged, and the canal will be tighter already. Because of this, the man's penis will be hugged closely as it slides in and out of her and this will make for extra pleasure for him.

Bend and Press

The 'bend and press' position gives the man control of the situation as the woman is lying back and receiving him. The woman will lie back on the floor or on the edge of the bed with her knees drawn up to her chest. The man then will stand close to her and slide his penis into her, leaning forward to hold her knees to her chest. This means that the woman does not have much freedom of movement, and the man is deciding the depth, the speed, and the angle at which his penis is entering her. He is likely able to achieve deep penetration in this position as her legs are lifted all the way to her chest and the man's body is holding them here, opening her body up for deeper penetration.

Legs on Shoulders

If the woman is feeling flexible and you want to try a new position that will have the man feeling great pleasure from a deeper penetration than most of the classics, try this one. The woman will lie on her back, and the man will lie on top of her, sliding his body in between her legs. Then, the woman will lift both of her legs so that each of them is on one of his shoulders. From here, he pushes his hips forward and can easily slide his penis into her vagina, which is open wide and in a perfect position for penetration. The man will do the thrusting here. This position requires flexibility from the woman but gives a deep penetration once accomplished. If she can't quite get both of her legs on his shoulders because of flexibility, she can start by lifting just one of them. She can put one leg on his shoulder and have the other one in a comfortable position beside him or around his waist. Having only one leg on his shoulder will still offer some of the benefits of deeper penetration and you can work up to lifting both legs eventually. The man will feel great pleasure from this deep penetration as the woman's legs are open for the deepest possible penetration.

The Scissors

This position is a little difficult to get yourselves into, but once you do, it will be well worth the effort. To begin, the man will sit on the bed with his arms behind him, holding his weight up but leaning back. Then, he will bend one of his knees, so his leg is bent. The woman will lie down on the bed face-down and with her head at the opposite end of the bed as the man's. She will spread her legs and move her body toward the man's body until their bodies meet. When they meet, their bodies will look like two pairs of scissors crossed into one another. From here, the man will insert his penis into her vagina. The woman can move her body up and down on his penis and the man can thrust into her. It may take a bit of time to develop a rhythm in this position, but when you do, you will both feel intense pleasure.

Tips for Better Female Pleasure

The Waterfall

The waterfall is a somewhat difficult position to get into, but once you do, it will be very pleasurable for the woman. In this position, the man has complete control, but this works in the woman's favor as he is able to focus on her entire body, leading to great amounts of pleasure for her. The man will begin by sitting in a chair with his feet on the floor. The woman will climb onto his lap, facing him, and insert his penis into her. She can wrap her legs around his waist. Then, slowly she will lean all the way back until her head and arms are touching the floor. From here, the man will hold onto her hips and can move her body onto his penis at whatever speed and depth he wishes. He can also grab onto her breasts and massage her clitoris in this position, which is what makes it so pleasurable for the woman. Not only is she receiving G-Spot stimulation because of the angle at which the man's penis is entering her, but she is also having her clitoris or nipples stimulated.

The Sitting Duck

The sitting duck is a position that allows the woman to have complete control. The man will lie down on the floor on his back. The woman will straddle him and slide his penis into her. Then, one by one, she will cross her legs so that she is essentially sitting on his penis cross-legged. In this position, the man has no freedom of movement, and everything is up to the woman. She can even touch her clitoris in this position if she wishes.

Being Sexual Without Doing It

Challenges

Phone Sex
Call your partner when you're separated for the night. Do not use the camera. Start touching yourself while speaking with your partner. Tell your partner what you'd like to do him right now, and he should respond with what he'd like to do for you.

Mirror Masturbation
Masturbate while your partner is masturbating herself/himself as well. Both must be naked and sitting across from each other, either on the opposite sides of the bed or in 2 chairs/sofas/etc.

Skype Sex
While separated, call your partner using FaceTime/skype. Start touching yourself while watching your partner enjoying the show as well. You can add some sex noise if you'd like to spice things up.

Sex Shopping
Go to a sex shop and buy a toy for your girl. Buy something that she'd like to try in bed. Don't be shy—ask the owner for help to find something recommended that will make your woman enjoy.

Hand job While Driving
Give your man a hand job while he is driving. Try to make him cum. If your husband is a bad driver, you can do this in a traffic jam.

20-Minutes of Kissing
For 20 minutes, do nothing but kissing passionately.

Sexting
Exchange at least 20 pictures with each other. Take your clothes off, wear sexy underwear, picture yourself in sexy positions on the bed, do whatever you'd like to make this challenge as sexy as you can.

Text Sex
When you're apart, have text sex. Start with explaining how you want to kiss... and then touch... and increase the temperature as your partner is seducing you with texts.

Read Erotica
When you're in bed together, pull up a nice erotica book, and read together. This can increase your sexual attraction, and you may find in common a lot of things that you find hot.

Striptease
Give your partner a special striptease show. If you aren't sure how to do it, simply watch some YouTube videos and learn. It doesn't have to be perfect—it's the intention that counts.

Never Have I Ever
Play 'never have I ever'. Start with general questions, and then narrow them down to sexual questions.

Remote Controlled Vibrator
Purchase a remote-controlled vibrator. Before you go out with your partner, ask her to put it in her panties. Play with the remote control in restaurants, in traffic jams, it's your choice!

Drive-thru
Make your partner cum while you're waiting in the line of a drive-thru.

Sex Club
Go to a sex club together. Make sure to respect the dress code. If you're too embarrassed, go to a club that allows masks.

Sex Dice
Purchase a pair of sex dice and play with them.

Special Piercing
Get a piercing together. Choose a place on the body that will turn you on.

Nipples Only
For 20 minutes, do nothing but playing with your partner's nipples.

Love Notes
This challenge is less about sex and more about romance, which can bond you better and spike attraction. Simply leave love notes for your partner, telling

them how much you appreciate, love, respect, and happy to be in a relationship with them.

The Naked Chef
Cook and eat a meal together, completely naked.

Download an App
The internet doesn't belong only to singles. Download those couple's apps: Happy Couple, Simply Us, Between, You & Me.

Swingers Party
Go to a swinger's party. If that is not your thing, you can just watch.

For Her

Step 1 Self-Sensory Examination

How:

This preliminary testing of your reactions to touch is essential before starting serious masturbation.

For this exercise you will need some kind of lubricant; you can use saliva, vaginal secretions, or a commercial lubricant or massage oil.

Complete privacy is very important. If at all possible, do this exercise while completely alone in the house. Take the phone off the hook and lock the door. Don't rush through this; take as much time as you need. The exercise usually takes about twenty minutes, but allow yourself plenty of leeways so you don't feel pressured to hurry up and finish before someone interrupts you.

Then draw a circle on your diagram to represent the pubococcygeus muscle in your vagina as a clock. Inserting your finger into your vagina, now test the sensations in your muscle. Find the muscle by putting the tip of your finger about halfway in and squeezing your vagina against your finger. Turn your finger in different directions as you squeeze, and you will feel the closing of a band around your finger. You may have to put your finger in farther or not so far to find this band, which is your pubococcygeus muscle. Rate on the diagram as follows for the sensory test of this muscle:

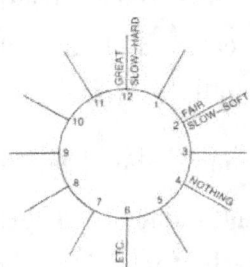

When you have tested each part separately, you are finished with the exercise. Do the exercise four or five times a week for as long as six weeks.

Why:

Discovering the sensations in different parts of your genitals before starting masturbation is important since successful masturbation involves knowing your genitals intimately—what they are, where they are, and how they feel when touched.

You must slow down enough to gather information in a nonstressful situation without seeking arousal or orgasm. Once you know more about your responses, you can then use this information toward those goals.

It is important to complete each step along the way. You feel you have waited too long already for your orgasm, but remember, you still have the rest of your life ahead of you. This is a learning process, which means you must take your time.

Step 2 Beginning Masturbation

How:

Although it may be difficult to arrange, you must be alone in the house when doing this exercise, or at any rate, without anyone around who is old enough to know what you are doing. This is true even for women who think they aren't self-conscious.

If you feel frazzled and tense when you are ready to begin this exercise, take a few minutes to unwind and relax first. If at all possible, try to pick your most energetic time of the day to do the exercise.

Using some lubricant and your hand, begin exploring your breasts, your external genitals, and your vagina, slowly and gently. Touch the different parts, individually and simultaneously. Caress both the major and minor labia, and slowly and gradually include the area around the clitoris, and finally the glans, the foreskin, and the shaft of the clitoris itself.

One suggestion for stimulating the breasts is to caress them in a slow, firm movement from the outer area toward the nipple. Then the nipple can be very lightly touched in a "teasing" manner. Alternate between breast and nipple stimulation, gradually increasing pressure directly on the nipple. Some women enjoy being almost pinched on the nipples, but this is usually after a gradual progression from breast to the nipple.

In touching the clitoris, it is important to remember the three parts—the shaft, which is the tubelike part below the mons; the glans, which is at the bottom of the shaft and looks like a tiny pea, and the foreskin, which is the hood or covering of the glans. If the foreskin covers the glans completely, it is necessary to retract it upward to expose the glans to direct touch. These three parts together constitute the clitoris.

The clitoris, like the breasts, can be stimulated in a variety of ways: with the thumb, forefinger, two or three fingers together, on the one hand, one finger of each hand at the same time, both thumbs, the palm or heel of the hand, the thumbnail or fingernail (lightly), or by using a small cloth to achieve friction. Touch can be in an up-and-down motion, from side to side, or in circular motions that are broad, short, or in between. You can touch from the bottom of the glans upward and over the shaft and from the shaft down over the glans. You can touch one side of the shaft or the glans or both sides together. (Do not, however, try to stimulate yourself by rubbing against an object such as a pillow. Although many women can become aroused in this manner, it is difficult to add vaginal stimulation to this method of masturbation.) Rhythm can be fast, slow, intermediate, or a combination and pressure can be light or firm, although, in the learning stage, it is usually preferable to start with a light touch and gradually increase it as desired.

For Him

Cockhead and Palm Series

This first series is surprising in more ways than one. You need to get used to a completely different hand position, but once you do, you'll keep returning to these for some great orgasms. Of the four in the series, the first three use a reverse handgrip over the front of your cock. The fourth one returns you to your customary fist grip.

NEW PLEASURE 1: Reverse Jerking with Cockhead Colliding into Palm

The emphasis in this technique is on the downward motion. Basically, you're concentrating on the lower half of your cock while your dick's most sensitive top is receiving stimulation through accidental collisions with your palm. This is a great way to prolong a delicious pre-orgasmic state. Of course, you'll only be able to stand it for so long and will just have to cum like crazy, especially with the more intense variation.

The initial setup is really important here. Your wrist and fingers will be pointing down; your rounded palm will be placed over your cockhead. This is how it's going to go:

6. Your hand wraps around the front of your cock with a couple of your fingertips and thumb positioned somewhere above or close to your balls.
7. You start jerking lightly with this reverse hand position, making sure your palm is rounded and positioned right over your dickhead but not quite touching it.
8. As you go on to jerking harder, your cockhead is going to keep bumping into your rounded palm.

A variation on Cockhead Collision. The setup and jerking action are nearly the same as above.

1. The only difference is that your hand wraps around the front of your cock quite a bit higher. Your fingertips and thumb, pointing down, are positioned no lower than an inch or two under the head.
2. As you go on to jerking harder, your cockhead will keep bumping into your curled fingers. This is going to feel pretty intense.
3. For even more intense sensation and truly explosive orgasm, you pause from time to time and squeeze your cock between all your fingers and thumb before returning to reverse jerking.

Sexual Energy

Think about a man who happens to be the leader of the pack. He's the guy that has a lot of drive, and he's also the guy that you don't really want to mess with. The man that you're thinking of is likely to be rather dominant in the workplace, and he also has a lot of success behind him, or it's clear he has a lot in front of him. A man such as this is likely to have a lot of sexual energy, simply because this is part of what drives him. But it's not only men who have this sexual energy, women do too, and they are also using it to their advantage.

As society starts to recognize that women are just as capable as men, employers are slowly taking on more women. This is indicative of a social change and the realization that this world doesn't just belong to men; it belongs to women too.

Whether you're a woman, a man, or you identify as being somewhere in between, you have sexual energy, and you can use it to your advantage no matter who you are, where you are, and what you do.

Anyone who has a lot of drive is likely to have a lot of sexual energy. If you want to have as much drive as others' have, then you need to work on your sexual energy.

Incredibly, you can use all of your sexual energy to help you transform many different areas of your life. I'm not just talking about getting ahead at work, I'm also talking about your personal life too.

Sexual Energy and Your Mind

Many people don't necessarily associate sexual energy with the mind, but these people are missing out. When you have sexual desire, you have a heightened state of sexual energy and arousal. This energy doesn't just affect your body; it affects your mind too.

Men know that once they've had sex, all they want to do is turn over and go to sleep. Men use up so much energy during sex that they need to rest. If you can refrain from having sex when you're aroused, you will have a sharper mind, and you won't feel the urge to go to sleep.

Women's sexual urges don't always 'Heat up' quite as quickly as a man does, but they do take longer to 'Cooldown'. Men and women may be different under the covers, but when it comes to their brains, they can use the power of sexual energy to make magic happen.

When the body is sexually stimulated, your brain will have no problem thinking and entering a level of consciousness that isn't ordinarily explored or taken advantage of. It's this level of consciousness and a heightened sense of awareness that you can use to your full advantage; you just have to know-how.

Take Those Feelings...

When you become sexually stimulated, take those feelings, and use that urge to have sex in a completely different way. When you reach this level of consciousness, you will automatically stop worrying about those trivial things you usually have on your mind. Instead, you will be able to focus, become a lot more motivated, and you'll even come up with ideas that you may not have thought of otherwise.

Now you may be wondering if this is really true or whether I'm simply making all this up. My friend, I say to you: Try it for yourself, and you will have the answer you need. Become sexually stimulated, and then focus on your business goals, your ambitions, and your ideas. Explore and feel what it's like to have that locked-in determination and focus that you may not have experienced before, and use it completely to your advantage.

Turn Them into Something Productive

It takes a lot of discipline to become sexually aroused and not do anything about it.

It doesn't matter how aroused you're feeling; you need to turn those feelings into something productive. As I said, this will take a lot of discipline, but it will become easier over time. As soon as you're used to turning these feelings around, you'll realize that you can make them work for just about anything you have in mind.

Become aroused, and then think about what you want to accomplish. Hold on to the feelings of arousal, and then think about what you want to do:

- Solve that work-related issue
- Draw or paint something amazing
- Come up with a great new project
- Win a tennis match

- ...and so on

Right now, you may be wondering how on earth you're going to achieve all this. The idea may seem quite alien to you now, but it can and will work if you give it a try. This may mean that you have to get yourself aroused if you don't have a partner, they don't want to participate, or you're someplace where you cannot get aroused easily. Find somewhere private, and do what you have to do in order to get aroused, and then put the plan into action.

I know that the idea of becoming aroused and using that energy elsewhere may seem strange, but it's one that can really transform your life. As with all new ideas, you will need to give this one a try a few times, before you can honestly and truly benefit from it. I encourage you to try this method, as it can take your mind and productivity levels to places you didn't know existed. After a while, it will all become second nature to you, and you'll wonder how you managed without it.

Sexual Energy and Spiritual Energy

Sexual energy and spiritual energy may be two different things to you. Sexual energy is that which drives us to make love, but spiritual energy is deemed to be something quite different.

The truth is that sexual energy and spiritual energy can be one and the same thing if you know how to change your energy and use it in a different light. Just as I have suggested that you use sexual energy to help you focus your mind, I also want to suggest that you use it to reach a more spiritual plane too.

Humans are sexual beings, and we exist in order to mate with others and increase the population. I know I'm looking at this from a very basic angle, but it's important to look at it this way if we are to understand our very being and why we are here. Humans are also spiritual beings, we're always looking for answers, and it's in our nature to search for a higher being.

Tell Your Partner Your Fantasies

Communication is the key to a fulfilling and pleasurable sex life. Knowing what you and your partner like and dislike allow you to focus on the things you enjoy and leave the things you don't behind. Knowing this will help to greatly reduce your anxiety surrounding performance or being able to please your partner adequately. With so many options for ways to pleasure each other, you don't want to waste time on the things that don't make you scream out in pleasure, and communication is the way!

Talking Before Sex

What You Both Like and Don't Like

In terms of sex acts, this could be anything like oral sex, fingering, anal, and other butt stuff or anything that she enjoys, no matter how big or small. These could be things she has tried before, wants to try in the future, has never tried before, or that she knows she does not want to try. Keep this question very open-ended to get the maximum amount of information possible.

What You Both Need and Like During Foreplay Specifically

This could include the length of time she needs, what acts she likes done to her, and what she likes to do to you during foreplay if she likes kissing to be included or not and what it takes to get her into the mood and wet enough for penetration.

What You Both Like and Don't Like Specifically That You Do Or Have Done

These are things specifically related to the two of you having sex with each other. The other questions in this list are open to including anything in her past and anything she has not yet tried. Try not to take it too personally if she tells you there is something she does not enjoy as much as you thought she did. This conversation is all about growth and learning.

What, if Anything, Makes You Both Orgasms Almost Instantly

Maybe something she does for herself during masturbation or something she knows will set her off instantly in the best way. This could be something you do for her or something she likes to do for herself.

What Both of Your Favorite Positions are

Her favorite sex positions, both for penetrative sex and for sex not involving penetration. What she likes about them would also be beneficial for you to know.

Any Kinks or Fetishes You Both May Have
Both that she has experience with and that she is just discovering. If she is unsure, ask her if she is open to exploring new kinks with you. Maybe you both will find new things that you really enjoy.

Anything You Both Have Wanted To Do Sexually Specifically With You
Maybe you have never done a 69 together, but she enjoys this position, or maybe she saw something in a porn video that she would like to try. Maybe there is something that she has wanted to experiment with, and she is wondering if you would be open to it.

Anything You Both Have Been Fantasizing About Trying
Maybe a role-play or a specific location, maybe a fantasy that she is embarrassed to talk about. This question is last on the list because hopefully, at this point, the conversation is flowing a little easier, and she will be more comfortable answering this question by now. Make her feel comfortable and let her know anything she discloses to you will remain between you and her.

While these questions are extremely personal, you will have to make each other feel comfortable being open about these topics. This will require a lot of vulnerability on both of your parts, so show your partner that you are listening intently and assure them that you are doing so without judgment. If they seem very hesitant to open up about these things- and they might be, depending on the age of your relationship and each of your levels of openness with sex in general, you can ask them if they would rather you answer the questions first, and they can answer them afterward. This may make them feel less like they are on the spot (especially if you were the one that brought it up) and more comfortable with the conversation as a mutual exchange.

Once you have begun to explore your sexual fantasies, kinks, and fetishes, you will be able to begin exploring them. There are many ways to try new things in the bedroom for the first time. Exploring your fetishes is a lifelong process, as your likes and desires may change over time. Once you have found out how to be in touch with this part of yourself, you can continue to let it enlighten your sex life forever.

When it comes to sex, communication is key to ensure everyone has a happy ending.

Your Path to Passion

Walk the Path Together

The Five T's and a Bit of Spice method is for women in relationships. This is because low sexual desire is something that generally occurs within the context of a long-term relationship. Also, because the vast majority of low-desire women are married, I use the word "husband." For example, I might say, "Talk with your husband about..." or "Do this exercise with your husband." Certainly, there are many women who are not married but who are in long-term relationships that have this same problem; if you are one of these women, I hope you will look past my use of the term husband and fill in the word or name that fits for you.

You might notice that I left culture, race, and religion out, even though many of the real-life examples are from women-of-color and from women from a variety of religious groups. The intersection of race, culture, religion, and sexuality deserves more attention, as do issues of sexuality for women with disabilities. Nevertheless, this written masterpiece is geared to address as wide an audience as possible: heterosexual coupled women who, regardless of their race, culture, economic status, religion, or age, currently feel too tired for sex and who want to find passion once again.

Getting as Much Passion as Possible from the Plan

There are a few general explanations and instructions that will help you get as much out of this masterpiece as possible. Following these instructions is going to increase your chances of feeling horny once again.

Focus on More Than Your Genitals

It is important for you to realize that not all of the techniques you will read about and try will be sexual. In fact, some are not sexual at all. You will especially find much nonsexual material in the Talk and Time steps. To illustrate, you will be encouraged to talk with your husband about your general needs. Learning to ask for your needs to be met about nonsexual matters will help you recover your sex drive in two ways. First, your needs will be better met so you won't be as depleted, giving you more energy for sex. Second, learning to ask for your needs to be met in nonsexual areas will help you learn to ask for them to be met sexually. Likewise, in the timestep, you will be encouraged to spend nonsexual, connected time with your spouse, and will be asked to start spending time exercising. Although neither activity is sexual, both are widely known among psychologists as activities that enhance women's sex drive. Women who have lost their sex drive due to stress and exhaustion are particularly in need of strategies that address these root causes. If you are too tired to have sex, you will need to address both your exhaustion and your sex drive. Your sex drive is part of your life and not just something that occurs in your clitoris and vagina. This written masterpiece does not take a genital approach to sex. It takes a whole-person approach, of which your genitals are just one part.

Sex Is More Than Intercourse

Just as sex involves more than just your genitals, your genitals need a lot more than just intercourse. While in popular language, the word sex has become synonymous with intercourse, sex is much more than penetration. For most women, penetration is not a sexual act that consistently results in orgasm. So, sex is meant in a broader way than intercourse. When referring to intercourse, this word will be used specifically. An important exception is when real women are quoted. In this case, the women's words have not been altered, even if they use the word sex to refer to intercourse. So, when describing these studies, the word sex is used except in those rare cases where researchers actually mention a specific sexual act such as intercourse. It is striking that even scientists fall prey to the notion that sex is synonymous with intercourse. Remember that sex involves so much more than this one specific sexual act.

Follow Your Desire

You are more likely to regain and hold onto your desire if you absorb this masterpiece slowly. Much of the information is best digested in chunks. This is why I often give exercises and then ask you to put the masterpiece down and try that exercise for a week. This also mimics the homework given in therapy.

You are rushed and stressed for the rest of your life, and this written work is not going to work if you approach it as one more thing to do quickly. To enjoy sex, you need to slow down and revel in the physical sensations. Likewise, to benefit most from this book, you need to unhurriedly take in the information and try the strategies. If you rush through this book by skipping exercises or doing the exercise in less time than suggested, you simply won't get as much benefit as you could.

Don't Become Disheartened

Some of you will resonate more with one portion of the program than others. For example, the sexual fantasies encouraged in the Thoughts step might get Amy's juices flowing again, but do nothing for Sally. Perhaps one of the ideas presented in the Touch step will begin to revive Sally's desire; perhaps Sally will feel a much-awaited throb of desire when her husband covertly rubs her inner thigh under the table the way he used to do. Try each of the steps but do not become disheartened if each and every step does not result in immediate effects. Keep on reading and keep on trying, and also remember that these strategies are tools for life that you can continue to come back to in order to keep your sex drive alive.

It is my sincere hope that each and every one of you will finish reading the written work with your sex drive back, but I know this isn't realistic. As a psychologist with more than twenty years of experience doing therapy, I know that problems are often more complex and multilayered than they initially seem. So, I must say at the outset that a few of you will complete the written work without fully recovering your drive. A few of you may be starting this written work thinking that your problem is being too tired for sex, and may find out that you have other issues contributing to your low desire. If this is the case, I will point you in other directions for seeking help. Appendix A explains how to find a good therapist and Appendix B recommends self-help written work on a variety of topics. Even if you end up discovering that you need additional help for problems not addressed by this written work, I am certain that what you learn here will give you the leg-up in dealing with these other issues.

The Women You Will Meet

I use genuine examples from both friends and clients throughout this written work. These people gave me their permission to use their stories—with the promise I would protect their identities. Thus, the names used are never real ones. At times, I change details to further conceal my sources. None of the examples are changed to the point of inaccuracy. My goal was to keep their identities anonymous while maintaining the integrity of each point or situation. My profound thanks go to the people who allowed me to depict the private details of their lives so that I could assist you.

We're Working Together!

As you read this, I want you to feel as if you are having a personal and useful talk with someone that you trust. Along these same lines, I will converse with you openly and honestly, in straightforward terms.

I will give you information and advice. I will ask questions to help you pinpoint the issues you are struggling with. I tell my therapy clients that we will work as a team, with my job being to provide information and expertise and their role being to provide the effort needed to think and act differently. The same applies here; together, we will work to help you recover your desire.

Cougar Unleashed

She's an upscale single lady living in a very private and exclusive gated community. Educated, sophisticated, and confident, she worked hard to excel in her profession and succeed in business. Her wealth enables her to live a comfortable lifestyle with enough luxuries to keep her mostly happy. However, there were a few desires she suppressed and left unsatisfied until now. Unfortunately, most of the men in her social circles are either committed to a wife, business, or another guy. But, the administration of her gated community offered a perk for single ladies they weren't even aware of. Every imaginable service was taken care of by a team of specialists. And, for security reasons, they provided a picture of all their staff for easy identification at the customer's door when they arrived. It was like they provided her with a catalog of potential playmates to fulfill all her fantasies. All she needed was a plausible reason to call for the type of help she desired. Being 'off-limits' made the seduction even more thrilling for both her and her prey. There's no point in having lots of money if you can't enjoy some naughty fun with it.

Improve Sexual Libido Adding Hypnosis Session

Hypnosis is a technique studied by M. H. Erickson to obtain direct "access" to the most intimate essences of the subconscious. It is a state of consciousness, causing an intense level of concentration directed on a single thought. This condition is obtained by resorting to a sensory stimulus such as a light, the therapist's voice, facilitate the induction of the mono section.

Therefore, it is not a state of sleep, nor of ecstasy; because the subject is conscious but in a different way than usual because it is magnetized by a particular attractive pole. As soon as one realizes that the hypnotic experience is indeed very pleasant, the resistances are reduced, the alarm is calmed, and levels of trance are started that are much more significant and useful. Sexuality can benefit a lot from this therapy.

Hypnosis can help that targeted psychotherapy called sex therapy, in which this conditioning is analyzed and overcome, making more rapid and lasting solution. Hypnosis plays an important therapeutic role in many situations of life, allowing reconstruction of a positive perception of self and gradually replacing it with the negative one caused by anxiety, and many forms of fears and inhibitions that are at the base of illnesses and discomforts, including sexual ones.

Male Sexual Disorders

Male sexual dysfunctions are characterized by clinically different discomfort with respect to the functionality of the subject of response to sexual stimulation and experience pleasure during intercourse. So, to include this distinction, one must use some tricks, as a lack of knowledge of sexuality and adequate stimulation could cause erroneous attributions. Sexuality is an integral part of the life of every individual.

Stages of the Sexual Report

Sexual intercourse is a complex experience that can be divided into four phases experienced by both men and women: desire, excitement, orgasm, and resolution. Based on the aforementioned subdivision it is possible to find phase / specific malfunctions.

Desire

It concerns the person's motivation and desire to share the intimacy and physicality of the sexual event. This phase is often not fulfilled, which is why sexual problems related to desire can arise. The latter is influenced by sexual "memory," which, stimulates desire and, therefore, greater satisfaction in the relationship. Stimulation of desire in man can take place through devices such as a situation in which the possibility of having a sexual relationship arises. During this phase, the penis rises and increases its size, which reaches its maximum during the phase of excitement. The body tends to its upper part, and redness often appears. The basis of sexual dysfunctions is undoubtedly the desire for an intimate relationship which, if absent, influences both excitement and orgasm, causing erection disorders, sexual pain, and orgasm disorders, such as premature or delayed ejaculation.

Excitement

It concerns the psychophysical sexual activation, or rather the tumescence of the penis and the consequent erection. In this phase is difficult for a man to maintain an erection until the end of the intercourse and the decrease in penile rigidity during the same. This inhibition could derive from living the relationship as proof of one's sexual abilities. Furthermore, prejudices about penis size could affect a man's identity and influence performance. Erectile dysfunction is connected to low self-esteem. Of course, also a couple of factors affect together with any physical and hormonal problems. This disorder is characterized by a lack or reduction of interest and sexual pleasure for a period of at least six months and is a source of discomfort for the person suffering from it. It could derive from relational problems.

Orgasm

The orgasm phase instead sees the achievement of the maximum sexual pleasure and consequent relaxation of the tension. Penis then ejaculates seminal fluid with rhythmic contractions of the muscles of the urethra. Finally, during the resolution phase, it loses its erection and returns to its normal size. Orgasm, the culmination of sexual intercourse, is a process that involves the whole body. Basically, it is the same in both sexes, however, the way it develops differs. Most men can get an orgasm through masturbation and generally reach it naturally during intercourse. Thus, a man's orgasm is an involuntary act, while in women, it is given by a voluntary physiological response. Male sexual disorders in this phase involve delayed ejaculation and premature ejaculation.

Delayed or Early Ejaculation

In the first case, there is a delay or absence of ejaculation. This condition is rarely found and attributable to factors of a psychological nature. Premature ejaculation is more common. It could derive from inexperience, interrupted coitus, hasty relationships, stress, or excessive use of erotic fantasies. In humans, pain can occur during erection, penetration, and ejaculation and can result from urological problems or penile malformations.

The Disorders of Sexual Pain

They interfere with various stages of sexual response. Today, an integrated approach is preferred in the treatment of sexual dysfunctions; that is an approach that puts mind and body on the same level, assuming that sexuality is an expression of both and therefore an affective-relational or somatic malfunction can result in sexual dysfunction.

Intervention Through Hypnosis

It is possible to define hypnosis as a state of relaxation in which a person comes into contact with his resources; therefore, sees alternative solutions to problems that he is unable to identify on a daily basis. Human sexuality is strongly influenced by self-suggestion which, if negative, can lead to a form of negative self-hypnosis, which in turn translates into sexual inhibition.

Sex therapy in hypnosis, therefore, allows us to work on those experiences that are prevented by an excessive level of anxiety. Among the goals of sex therapy in hypnosis, we see the development of the person's resources, the increase in sexual availability, and the facilitation of psychological and somatic modifications.

Hypnosis to Act on the Erectile Dysfunction

One of the male sexual disorders resulting from negative self-produced images is erectile dysfunction in the sexual arousal phase. The goal of hypnosis will be to reduce anxiety through the suggestion that leads the patient to enjoy an exciting situation without sexual pretensions, replacing the image of the flaccid penis with that of the erect penis.

Hypnosis for Orgasm Disorders

In orgasmic disorders instead, experts work on the conflict that inhibits orgasm in order to improve the reception of sexual reactions. In the male orgasm, hypnotic suggestion techniques are used to restore the sensitivity of the penis and fully experience sexual intercourse. Hypnosis is used with the aim of eliminating the negative images connected to the same allowing voluntary adjustment of the ejaculatory reflex.

Sex Therapy in Hypnosis—Defeating Female Sexual Dysfunctions

Female sexuality has been sacrificed for some time, as a woman is often indoctrinated in such a way as to perceive sexuality as uniquely necessary, therefore in this private perspective from the pleasure inherent in sexual intercourse. A good relationship with one's body and one's sexuality makes it possible to experience greater psycho-physical and relational well-being. It is possible to find a series of female sexual dysfunctions connected to the phases of the sexual response cycle, namely desire, excitement, orgasm, and resolution.

Every woman is different from the other, so sensory awareness and sexual reaction depend on a peculiar psycho-physical condition, as well as on the stimulation she receives from her partner or masturbation. The feminine desire revolves more around fantasies concerning relationships or the exchange of effusions. There are many reasons why female sexual desire is less strong than that of men, for example, because women often have difficulty reaching orgasm, or because they are afraid of feeling pain during sexual intercourse.

Lack of desire implies the impossibility of feeling sensations of excitement and, therefore, of experiencing orgasmic pleasure. The reaction is a passive attitude of the woman towards the partner and a consequent lack of communication in the couple. The absence of sexual desire in women could also occur as hormonal imbalances during the puerperium and menopause, leading to an inhibition of sexual fantasies. In this case, it is possible to find female hypoactive sexual desire disorder, or lack- reduction of sexual desire.

During this phase, stimulated by caresses, genital stimulation, skin odor, erotic fantasies, the genital organs are filled with blood; just like the penis, the small lips, and the clitoris swell, the vagina expands and happens vaginal lubrication. Therefore, the female organ is sensitized. In the phase of excitement, there is the persistence of muscular tension, in which the two inner thirds of the vagina relax, the breasts become turgid, and muscles around genital organs enter in tension. Clitoris enters an erection, exactly like its masculine equivalent, until it reaches the stage of orgasm, in which the muscles of the vagina, vulva, and anus contract rhythmically, resulting in a state of pleasure.

Following the last vaginal contraction, the resolution phase occurs in which the muscles regain their status, and the clitoris resumes its usual dimension. The stimulation to reach orgasm varies by nature and intensity in every woman, therefore, various ways are introduced through which to amplify the pleasure, from varying moment and place where one usually makes love to change position. Relaxation is certainly one of the fundamental factors of sexual pleasure, so a nervous woman during sexual intercourse will most likely not be able to fully enjoy it. Pleasure in the female sex is strengthened by the love and tenderness perceived in the bond with the partner. This is evidenced by the fact that women who live stable relationships tend to experience a more satisfying sex life than those who have only spaced and occasional relationships.

Another factor to keep in mind is the menstrual cycle that has an influence on the intensity of orgasm. Women are in fact more receptive during the ovulation period, that is fourteen days before the next menstrual period and during the night since the relationship gives relief from tension and fatigue. In this phase, disturbance of female orgasm could occur, given by persistent difficulty in reaching the orgasm or by a delay of the same. The dysfunction is such only if the woman recognizes her as a source of discomfort, as she may not complain of sexual dissatisfaction despite anorgasmia.

Further dysfunctions are related to sexual pain. An example is a dyspareunia, pain in genital organs during sex. Through inducing relaxation, it is possible to reach a state of psychophysical safety. In female anorgasmia, a journey through one's body is induced involving genitals. Through the imaginative exploration of the vagina, a woman experiences sexual pleasure by visualizing it in something concrete that then becomes the image of the partner. Finally, compared to sexual pain disorders, it is possible to use muscle relaxation and control techniques that allow management of anxiety related to penetration.

Conclusion

Trying new sex positions is recommended for couples. However, it is important to understand the importance of the problems that are related to the sex position before having sex. The advantage of the said position is that it is going to give you the utmost pleasure during sex.

Fortunately, there is actually more than one sex position that could be used for such a thing. Look at the one that could help your particular situation. Since every person has different body types you are going to need to take that into consideration as well. This means you are going to have to pick a sex position that has the best chance of actually working for you. Being prepared is a good idea, as well.

The first reason is the fact that it is going to work. That is important to keep in mind. Fortunately, there are a few things you are going to want to take into consideration. First and foremost, if you are thinking about making love in various sex positions, then you should definitely consider the problem with anal sex positions. You will want to think about how easy they are to do as well.

It all comes down to the position that you decide to engage in. The orgasm that you get from the position will be better than you would have gotten from the majority of other positions given the fact that you can actually relax during orgasm. If this is what you are looking for, then remember to think about the issue of bondage. It is a great method of giving the person pleasure during sex, while at the same time, not feeling entirely bad about it.

You are going to want to forget about that for right now, though. Try to go into it knowing that you know you are doing it to satisfy. It needs to be something that is exciting for you, exciting for the person you are with, and exciting for both of you as well. If you can do all of that, then you can actually have a good experience. Make sure that you take your time. Work at it a little bit. This is something that you are going to want to relax, meaning that you are going to need to try and work at finding out what your partner is truly into. That means working to understand what they like. It is going to take a little bit of time, but if you work at this, you can have a really enjoyable experience.

Remember to pay attention to your partner, though. Listen to them, and try to understand what they are saying and what they are asking for. You don't have to do exactly what they ask for. But the idea that you can keep them happy is something that is going to be very important if you are looking to be able to satisfy them.

But they are not telling you that you are not good enough. It is just a matter of your partner being able to get the most pleasure. The best way to make them happy is to listen to them and then work with them. You are going to find out quickly which sex positions work best for your partner. This is going to be the biggest difference. Quite a few partners have found that this is a great way to kind of relax and easily find a sex position that works for you both.

www.ingramcontent.com/pod-product-compliance
Lightning Source LLC
Chambersburg PA
CBHW071631080526
44588CB00010B/1354